Architecture as Signs and Systems

For a Mannerist Time

THE WILLIAM E. MASSEY SR. LECTURES IN THE HISTORY OF AMERICAN CIVILIZATION

Architecture as Signs and Systems

For a Mannerist Time

Robert Venturi & Denise Scott Brown

THE BELKNAP PRESS OF HARVARD UNIVERSITY PRESS · CAMBRIDGE, MASSACHUSETTS · LONDON, ENGLAND · 2004

Book Design by Peter Holm, Sterling Hill Productions

Library of Congress Cataloging-in-Publication Data

Venturi, Robert.
Architecture as signs and systems : for a mannerist time / Robert Venturi and Denise Scott Brown.
p. cm. – (The William E. Massey, Sr. lectures in the history of American civilization)
Includes bibliographical references and index.
ISBN 0-674-01571-1 (alk. paper)
1. Symbolism in architecture. 2. Communication in architectural design. I. Scott Brown, Denise, 1931- II. Title. III. Series.

NA2500.V45 2004
720'.1—dc22   2004040313

RV: To the memory of my artistic, intellectual and beloved parents and my brilliant friend, Everett DeGolyer; and to Philip and Kitty Finkelpearl, friends over the years who gave scholarly and aesthetic guidance, and to Akio Izutsu, friend and mentor in Japan.

DSB: To the memory of Ziona Cohen, Paul Davidoff, Jane Galansky, J. B. Jackson, Arthur Korn, Lily Lakofski, Phyllis Hepker Lakofski, Shim Lakofski, Manfred Marcus, Dorothy Pargiter, Charles Seeger, Doris V. Thompson, and Rosa Van Gelderen; and to David Crane and Herbert Gans. All were mentors and nurturers, concerned for me.

RV, DSB: To the memory of Steve Izenour. To our colleagues and students, the intersection of whose lives with ours can be traced in these pages. To everyone at VSBA and its ancestor firms, 1964–2004, and to Dan McCoubrey, Nancy Rogo Trainer, and Jamie Kolker, navigators for its future. To Jim Venturi—our beloved son.

— PREFACE —

This book is based on the The William E. Massey Sr. Lectures in the History of American Civilization, which we were invited to give at Harvard in 2003. We were told it was an opportunity to look back on our careers and to explain our interests to an educated lay public. The terms were to be personal and autobiographical. Nathan Glazer, who initiated the invitation, may have divined that we were at an appropriate stage in our lives for a recounting.

Lectures in architecture tend to go on and on. But architects tie their comments to illustrations; this helps to counteract the length, and it illuminates the abstract through the concrete. So in our lectures we showed slides of buildings, cities, and our own work and talked about our ideas. In the architecture tradition, slides were shown in pairs. The comparison helps to explain a concept or to build an argument.

This lecture format has dictated the working of this book. Pictures and writing go together—the photo-essay is our medium of choice. Faced with a photo-essay, some people look at the pictures and read the captions, while others skip the pictures and read the text. Both will find themselves at a loss here, where the captions are frequently part of the text, and the one may make no sense without the other.

Because our ideas have been a long time growing, some have appeared elsewhere in earlier forms. Portions of both Part I and Part II were presented at a symposium on our work titled, "In Your Face," given in New York on September 29, 2001, under the aegis of *Metropolis* magazine. The ideas in Chapter 8 are enlargements upon thought presented in "Talking about Context," *Lotus* 74, November 1992. More on the ontogeny of our ideas can be learned from our website, www.vsba.com, particularly from its bibliography. We have maintained this bibliography over the years as an offering to architectural scholarship, so we would be interested to hear from scholars and others of works we have missed.

In two long lives there are hierarchies of acknowledgment and thanks. Bob and I have tried, through the dedications in our books, to commemorate some important, heartfelt relationships, and that practice continues in the present dedication.

In the text, where they pertain, we mention colleagues who have taught us or helped us engender the ideas under discussion. A broader list of people who are linked to ideas in this book would include, for Bob's early years at Princeton: Donald Drew Egbert and Sherley W. Morgan, whose nourishing appreciation supported Bob from the onset of his life in architecture, and who have continued as a presence for him beyond their death. And at the American Academy in Rome: Richard Krautheimer, who shared his insights on Early Christian and Baroque architecture. And Philip Finkelpearl, whose understanding of Mannerism in literature helped sharpen Bob's understanding of Mannerism in architecture. And Vincent Scully, the first to see value in Complexity and Contradiction and whose support has continued over the years. For my early years at Penn, great teachers and thinkers in the Planning Department: G. Holmes Perkins, William G. Wheaton, Robert B. Mitchell, Chester Rapkin, Britton Harris, and Walter Isard. Martin Meyerson had left Penn by the time I arrived, but he was an unseen presence there, and has popped up ever since, an *eminence grise*, in the situations of our work life, up to and including today.

Tied to our professional lives as friends and advisors: Thomas and Agatha Hughes, Vincent Scully, Sydney and Frances Lewis, Elise Jaffe and Jeffrey Brown, George Thomas, Nicholas Gianopulos, Morris Kellett, Barney Horowitz, Stanhope and Libby Browne, and Paul Putney. Another hearty thanks goes to the scholars and students over the years who have searched us out to interview us, write about us, or just compare notes. It's heartening that owing, probably, to our website and bibliography, there are so many more of them these days—and from worldwide—and they have read so much more of what we have written than in earlier years.

Also in this book are credits to hundreds of hard-working individuals who have joined our offices in Philadelphia over five decades, and to our associated architects, clients, and photographers. Judith Glass and John

Izenour were pillars of strength in the making of the book. They were supported by Monica Vandergrift, Jeremy Tenenbaum, Lauren Jacobi, Sue Scanlon, and Matt Morong in organizing the material with understanding, skill, and diligence.

And then, there are our good friends, old and young, from many countries and related to diverse aspects of our lives—more than we can ever mention. Thank you for your love.

Although Bob is the author of Part I and I am the author of Part II, the content of this book derives from our joint work in research and design and from our collaboration of almost forty-five years. I introduced Bob to the significance of the everyday-ordinary, which he originally acknowledged in the last part of *Complexity and Contradiction in Architecture*, and I "corrupted" him (as he says) by inviting him to visit Las Vegas in 1966. Bob introduced me to the comparative and analytic techniques of scholarship in architectural history, and to the fun of applying them to the artistry of Las Vegas.

Although we were originally practitioners and teachers, we decided later to be practitioners and writers and thereby not diminish our focus on building and planning and, as Bob says, work with God in the details. Although each of us has evolved, as architect and theorist, out of a particular background, we have not worked explicitly to invent a school and promote our ideas thereby. As far as movements and schools in architecture are concerned, we have been loners—a pair of loners.

In writing about our lives, we risk the misunderstanding that we are writing autobiography. We are not. We are describing ideas from many sources. We've used our lives as a means of explaining them and showing how they feed our architecture.

DENISE SCOTT BROWN

— CONTENTS —

Introduction / 1
ROBERT VENTURI AND DENISE SCOTT BROWN

I Architecture as Sign rather than Space
  New Mannerism rather than Old Expressionism
  ROBERT VENTURI
    1. An Evolution of Ideas / 7
    2. Communication and Convention for an Iconographic
       Architecture / 12
    3. Architecture as Sign in the Work of VSBA / 41
    4. A New Mannerism, for Architecture as Sign / 73

II Architecture as Patterns and Systems
  Learning from Planning
  DENISE SCOTT BROWN
    5. Some Ideas and Their History / 105
    6. Activities as Patterns / 120
    7. The Redefinition of Functionalism / 142
    8. Context in Context / 175
    9. Essays in Context / 182
    10. Mannerism, Because You Can't Follow All the Rules of All
        the Systems All the Time / 212

Conclusion: Signs and Systems for a Mannerist Architecture for Today / 218
ROBERT VENTURI AND DENISE SCOTT BROWN

Notes / 225
Bibliography / 231
Illustration Credits / 235
Acknowledgments / 242
Index / 247

— INTRODUCTION —

Robert Venturi

An architect was heard to observe, after one of our recent lectures, that we had not had a new idea in forty years. My silent reaction was, of course, at least we'd had an idea.

But since then I have come to realize that what he said might be partly right, and not totally bad. Denise Scott Brown and I have had a few ideas, not a lot, and not completely new, but we hope they were good ideas. They have evolved over time, rather than changed with the fashions. We have not tried to bring out something new every month. Rather, we have acknowledged evolution as well as revolution within the development of architecture and its ideas.

Viva developing old ideas as well as discovering new ideas! *Viva* engaging a few slowly growing ideas over promoting lots of fleeting ideas! *Viva* pragmatic/evolutionary over heroic/revolutionary! In this era when "change and audacity have become ends in and of themselves," epiphanies in architecture worry me as much as vision in architecture.[1] To quote Marcel Proust: "The only true voyage of discovery . . . would be not to visit strange lands but to possess other eyes."[2] Or remember T. S. Eliot:

> We shall not cease from exploration
> And the end of all our exploring
> Will be to arrive where we started
> And know the place for the first time.[3]

Denise Scott Brown

Eliot's is an elderly person's observation. And in these essays, perhaps we, like him, arrive where we started and know that place, if not for the first time, then in another way.

Robert Venturi and I have had nearly four decades to see the results of our thought in our work. Although at one time Bob's mother's house was visible on the roofs of high-rise buildings worldwide, it has seen a slower, less apparent fruition in our own work. Yet I personally believe it cracked ajar every door in architecture that we have since opened. You can find it in our hotel in Japan, our unbuilt Whitehall Ferry Terminal, and our Life Sciences complex at the University of Michigan. The same holds for our "learning from" research.[4] Over the years we have given perhaps a half dozen answers to the question, "What did you learn from Las Vegas?" and none is final.

As makers and doers, our process is triangular: we look and learn; write and theorize; design and build. We jump from one to the other in no good order and need all three to produce our work. I have been a circus horse rider between my two professions, architecture and urban planning, most of my life. This position has its ups and downs, and I have perhaps needed a shot of mannerism to interpret its contradictions. But delving for ideas in areas of planning where architects seldom go has been fecund for me and instructive and invigorating for our architecture. In my essays I match planning thought, particularly urban social and economic theories, against some traditional notions of architecture, to see what richness the one can bring the other. I offer the combination as a portfolio of ideas that can contribute to humane and creative design, and I try to show how they have informed our architecture.

Riding the horses of practice and education as well, I have been intrigued by the differences between academic education, taught in much of the university, and professional education, taught architects and planners (also engineers, lawyers, and physicians). Practitioners use academic knowledge for purposes different from those of academics—to do things, to recommend policy, to take part generally in a world of action. The professional gets the fun of both learning *and* doing—and, if lucky, the reward of seeing the results. Therefore, I am addicted to practice, where this mainly happens.

In this book, I try, by professionalizing the academic, to broaden the repertory of thought available to architects in designing and to share some tools I have found valuable. This is difficult. Architects are as scared of the social sciences as social scientists are scared of the arts, and each stereotypes the other as lacking relationship with their interests. I have found that one way to help architects get beyond this barrier is to personalize the professional—to tell the story of pertinence through showing how those ideas crept into my own history. I think my students may have felt, "If Denise likes it, maybe I will too"—at least they seemed to want to share the images I enjoyed. So when I draw on my work and experience to illustrate my themes, it's not rambling reminiscence; my saunter through my life is to make the content of my thought understandable and palatable.

Bob, too, in his essays, shows his experience as a source of his work. Therefore, the sequences of our lives provide, to some extent, content and structure for this book and comparability in the two parts of it. Our essays move from Bob's profound take on one subject—architecture as sign—to my attempts to loosen the tight belt of architecture by bringing to it more than is in its present philosophies. In each part, a series of ideas is surveyed, at first historically and anecdotally, then as a set of themes relevant to architecture. These are illustrated through reference to historical architecture; urban maps, diagrams, and pictures; and examples of our own work. For the most part, the same few buildings are illustrated from chapter to chapter but each time from a different point of view, related to the theme of the chapter. We hope this evokes the multilayered quality of architecture and leads logically to the discussion on mannerism that ends each part of the book and is also the subject of the concluding chapter.

Where the references may be useful, we adopt the footnotes and attributions of formal learning, but we have tried to keep the tone of our writing colloquial and reachable, and also to show the passion that drives us. Readers may share the passion—though our idea is not to make others love what we love but rather to include passion in the professional.

We point out that we both share in and are responsible for *all* the subject matter of the book—in both its discovery and its adaptation. There is apparent redundancy in our two parts—in "Context in Context," for example, and in a few repeated illustrations—but the idea is to show his take and mine on various subjects. Together we make a career.

My attribution problems have continued since I described them in *Learning from Las Vegas* and "Room at the Top?"[5] I am still called "that architect" by planners and "that planner" by architects. Because most of my life exists in architecture, the second is a greater problem. Despite my training and practice, architects have difficulty allowing me to be an architect at all, let alone a designer. The facts are that, for some of our most complex projects, the partis evolved during our planning studies, long before we had architectural contracts. I have continued with these through subsequent phases, because I love to do so but also because if I don't follow up as far as the hinges on the doors, our coffee lounges won't be public.

Those who penetrate to the end of this book will see, I hope, the complementarity in our ideas and how working together makes us stronger—just as the collaboration over the years of the hundreds of people who have worked with us has added immensely to the quality of our work and the liveliness of our firm. Few people, however, give credibility to the notion of joint artistry in architecture. You decide.

Architecture as Sign rather than Space

New Mannerism rather than Old Expressionism

Robert Venturi

— 1 —
An Evolution of Ideas

In the medium of architecture, if you can't do it, you have to write it, and you can't do it if you are an architect ahead of your time. So I have felt a certain urgency in writing this book to get a couple of architectural ideas out that perhaps have not yet come into their own—ideas of Architecture as Sign rather than Space, and architecture that engages the manner of Mannerism. I can refer to lots of work from our office over decades acknowledging iconography, but not to work engaging in its manifestation the electronic technology that is relevant for our time. So here is that idea for the record—on record, if not in stone: architecture as sign (rather than space) for a mannerist (rather than expressionist) time.

But first, I want to glance backward at some ideas—mostly evolutionary—that have led up to, and provided background for, the current themes that are the subject of these essays:

Context in Architectural Composition
This was the subject of my master's thesis delivered in 1950, based on Gestalt psychology's notion that meaning is derived from context—an architectural idea revolutionary in a time when both Frank Lloyd Wright and Le Corbusier agreed that you design "from the inside out" and not, at the same time, from the outside in. Since then, my approach has been much acknowledged, but also much misunderstood and simplistically exploited, especially by bureaucratic design review boards who don't understand that contextual harmony can derive from contrast as well as from analogy, as my great teacher Jean Labatut taught me.

Complexity and Contradiction in Architecture
This book—published in 1966 and over the years translated into eighteen languages—is still in print as a revolutionary reaction to ideological purity and to the minimalist aesthetic and modular consistency

characteristic of late Modernism.[1] The book employs historical reference within a method of comparative analysis—the latter often profoundly misunderstood as a kind of promotion of stylist revival. Ideas within the idea of this book include "Less is a bore," "messy vitality," "both-and rather than either-or," and "Main Street is almost all right."

Michelangelo's Porta Pia (which could be referred to as *mannerissimo*) is illustrated on the cover of the second edition, and the revolutionary thesis of *Complexity and Contradiction* evolves within the book you are reading now as the idea of a mannerist architecture for our time. Which leads me to wonder (alas!), could the *expressionistic* complexity and contradiction characteristic of today's architecture be a misunderstood derivation from the *mannerist* complexity and contradiction I wrote about in that 1966 book?

Learning from Las Vegas

The subject and title of this book—co-authored with Denise Scott Brown and Steven Izenour, published in 1972, and still in print in several languages—represents perhaps an evolution from the concept of form, which was essentially the subject of *Complexity and Contradiction*, to symbolism, a revolutionary idea in the context of its time.[2] The Las Vegas described here is the commercial strip of c. 1968, not the scenographic Disneyland configurations of Las Vegas today. In an era dominated by aesthetic abstraction as well as vehicular urban sprawl, when both symbolism and commercial signage were scorned, our message was "*Viva* meaning rather than expression!" and what we referred to as "the duck and the decorated shed." Our current acknowledgment of architecture as Sign rather than as Space represents a kind of evolution beyond *Learning from Las Vegas*.

Iconography and Electronics upon a Generic Architecture

This book—published in 1996, still in print in English and Japanese, and about to be translated into Italian—represents an evolutionary development of the idea and significance of symbolism and signage acknowledged in *Learning from Las Vegas*.[3] But it is accompanied by a revolutionary idea: the relevance of electronic technology over industrial technology for the architecture of a Post-Industrial Information Age. In the end, this revolutionary idea will evolve into a form of changing communication engaging digital media at an architectural and urban scale—appropriate for today's multicultural world.[4]

And then within this book there is our acknowledgment of generic loft architecture as a valid framework for an architecture as signage.

And from here have evolved in our work, over time, two kinds of ideological ideas, which can be thought of as *perverse* and *positive*.

Perverse or Positive?

- *Perverse* where accommodation to context has come to mean over the last fifty years "Make the new look like the old," through the impositions largely of Community Design Review Boards.
- *Perverse* where acknowledgment of complexity and contradiction has come to mean "Make of the architecture of today articulated sculpture which is original/dramatique/ expressionist" and where the generic loft is outré.
- *Perverse* where complexity and contradiction in architecture, deriving from the method of historical reference, have been misinterpreted as justifying historical-revival Postmodernism.
- *Perverse* where the iconographic urbanism of a 1968 Las Vegas has evolved into the scenographic urbanism of today. But . . .
- *Positive* where the electrical signage exemplified by the Las Vegas Strip can evolve into electronic iconography for an architecture as sign.
- *Positive* where an architecture of complexity and contradiction which was *implicitly* mannerist can become an architecture that is *explicitly* Mannerist—in keeping with our current perversely complex and contradictory era, our neo-Byzantine era.

These last two evolutionary ideas I shall describe in the chapters that follow.

Context in Context—Embracing Dissonance

But first, via a kind of ungentle manifesto, I will touch on context in architecture and urbanism—the subject I introduced over fifty years ago and an element that dominates architectural thinking and process today.

- *Context* is an essential architectural element because meaning can derive from context, as Gestalt psychology emphasized.
- *Context* is important because it acknowledges the quality of a place, of a whole beyond the single building, and enhances an extended unity.
- *Context* does not mean the new has to look like the old—the old architectural vocabulary or urban composition or symbolic vocabulary.
- *Harmony in context* can derive from contrast as well as from analogy. (You can wear a gray suit with a gray necktie or a gray suit with a red necktie and engage perceptual harmony.)
- *Dissonance in context*, as well as lyricism—as in the dissonant chords within the symphonic works of Beethoven— can engage tension within the composition. (You can also wear a gray suit with a gray necktie that has red polka-dots and thereby engage dissonance— and mannerism.)
- *Complexity engages a range of contexts:* cultural, aesthetic, sociological, urbanistic, rather than just the formal or ideological.

All these points must be acknowledged as relevant at a time when hundreds of bureaucratic design review boards and committees pervade our Kafka-esque era, persecuting architects and stultifying architecture, and when the valid ideal of community participation in urban planning has in the end succumbed largely to the imposition of special interests. In *that* context, let us not forget our First Amendment rights, which promote, in addition to freedom of speech, freedom of *expression*—artistic expression as well as verbal expression. *A bàs* fascist unity! *Viva* vulgar, or at least messy, vitality! Zoning restrictions, Yes. Ideological dominance, No.

A manifestation of context at an urban scale which we consider particularly revealing is the typical American gridiron system of city planning. Established in the seventeenth-century plan of William Penn's Philadelphia, this is a prime example of a particularly American—and a particularly valid—kind of urban contextualism, one which engages contrast as well as analogy, dissonance as well as unity, and ends up pragmatic/dynamic rather than ideological/utopian. One where each of the streets extends to an infinite frontier rather than terminating axially and hierarchically at the equivalent of a ducal palace. One where the consistency of the gridiron street plan is balanced by an architectural individuality *within* the blocks and *along* the streets that engages valid and vital chaos. In this plan—where across the street from the mayor's house one can buy lunch in a delicatessen—order *and* democracy evolve. A building's significance derives not from its position relative to other buildings but from its inherent architectural quality, as expressed in form, scale, and symbolic content.

There can be wonderful exceptions within this framework— for example, in the juxtapositions of diagonally placed avenues extending to regional areas, as in Philadelphia's Baltimore Pike or Chester or Lancaster Avenues; or, in Washington, D.C., Pierre Charles L'Enfant's juxtaposition, upon an American gridiron system, of a series of diagonal axial avenues with architectural terminations, which create an element of hierarchy appropriate for a national capital.

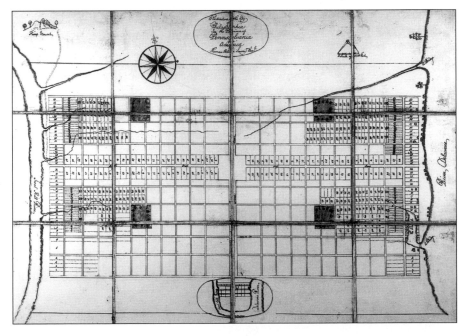

1. Seventeenth-century plan of William Penn's Philadelphia.

— 2 —
Communication and Convention for an Iconographic Architecture

As the implicit mannerism acknowledged in *Complexity and Contradiction* has evolved in our work into an explicit Mannerism for today, so has the Architecture of Signs and Symbols acknowledged in *Learning from Las Vegas* evolved (via *Iconography and Electronics upon a Generic Architecture*) into an architecture of communication for our time—an architecture explicitly embracing symbols and cultures that are both high and low, as demonstrated by our modification of Thomas Cole's *Architect's Dream*. (The original painting acknowledged architecture as form and symbol; the modified version acknowledges the cultures of architecture—high and low.) Here is Architecture as Sign, rather than Architecture as Space. Here is architecture for an Information Age, rather than architecture for an Industrial Age.

Here is architecture engaging:

- Iconographic Surface, rather than Articulated Form
- Explicit Communication, rather than Artistic Expression
- Iconography, rather than Abstract-Expressionism
- Electronic Technology, rather than Electrical Games
- Digital Splendor, rather than Gloomy Glow
- Changing Varieties of Messages and Ornament—to accommodate Multiculturalism—rather than Abstract Purity
- Convention—acknowledging Everyday-Ordinary—rather than Original-Dramatique
- Generic Vernacular Shelter, rather than Exotic Expressionist Sculpture
- Evolutionary Pragmatism, rather than Revolutionary Ideology
- Mannerist Multimedia, rather than Expressionistic Purity

2. Thomas Cole's *The Architect's Dream.*

3. *The Architect's Dream* augmented by VSBA.

And including thereby:

- Vernacular Commercial Architecture as Sign—as Vital and Valid—rather than just Vulgar
- Valid Urbanism, acknowledging automobile transportation as well as public transportation

RECENT PRECEDENTS AND CURRENT FASHION AS CONTEXT FOR ARCHITECTURE AS COMMUNICATION

Classic Modern architecture of the early and mid-twentieth century is a valid precedent for our time. It engaged (implicitly but not explicitly, and ironically but not manneristly) ideal if contradictory combinations of abstract form on the one hand and of industrial symbolism on the other. Its ideological functionalism prescribed designing from the inside out, with no accommodation to context or with an assumption of context as being inevitably an ideal kind of park—but never a parking lot! Le Corbusier's Villa Savoye (my favorite building of the twentieth century) is the prototype of this period: it engages eloquently abstract form and space in a parklike setting, whose composition becomes a kind of Mondrian painting par excellence (but without Mondrian's use of color!) and exemplifies Le Corbusier's famous definition of architecture as being "the masterly, correct and magnificent play of masses brought together in light."[1]

The ironical industrial symbolism of that period was promoted by Le Corbusier in his significant writing, especially in *Vers une Architecture* of 1923, where he specifically and enthusiastically celebrated America's late nineteenth- and early twentieth-century industrial vernacular architecture (he especially loved midwestern grain elevators).[2] As early as 1909 Walter Gropius had already adapted an industrial vocabulary for his Fagus Shoe Works. Le Corbusier's later vocabulary—equally influential—engaged *béton brut*, which was abstract in its ultimate aesthetic, involving heavy rather than light form, combined with another kind of industrial reference.

4. Le Corbusier's Villa Savoye, Poissy, France.

5. Piet Mondrian's *Composition with Red, Blue, and Yellow.*

6. Grain elevators, from Le Corbusier's *Towards a New Architecture.*

7. Walter Gropius's Fagus Shoe Works, Alfeld-an-der-Leine, Germany.

A significant exception to the dominance of abstraction within the Modernist aesthetic of the last century occurs in the architecture of the Russian Constructivists, which teems with iconographic signs integral to the building. This graphic–symbolic exception corresponds to imagery that is industrial within abstract mainstream Modernism.

These architectural precedents contrast vividly with the architecture I describe as relevant for today, but they were essentially valid for their time. When we turn to early Modern urban design rather than architecture, what we find is invalid—revolutionary/utopian at all costs rather than evolutionary/pragmatic. This is exemplified by Le Corbusier's Ville Radieuse, which

8. Constructivist designs.

9. Le Corbusier's Ville Radieuse.

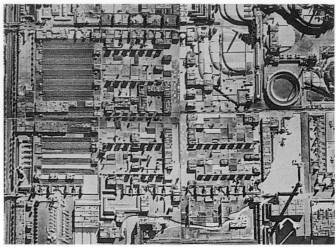

10. Frank Lloyd Wright's Broadacre City.

proposed the demolition of the center of Paris except for the Isle de la Cité and a few buildings like the Panthéon and the church of the Sacré Coeur. Or by Frank Lloyd Wright's equally simplistic purist ideal as expressed in the snobbish/segregated suburbanism of Broadacre City or the pompous megastructural urbanism for Pittsburgh Point.

May I now suggest that an architecture afflicts us in our own time that is the equivalent of the city planning that afflicted us fifty years ago—heroic-original, purist-utopian, extravagant (both aesthetically and cost-wise), and invalid within the context of Architecture as Communication? I refer to the superficially Complex and Contradictory manner that distinguishes the Neomodern style of today—with its metallic combinations of exposed Victorian trusses, sagging/decorative guy wires, and obsolete/decorative rivets—the latter symbolizing exotic teats, as a perverse equivalent of Classical egg-and-darts ornament? *Viva* electronic pixels over decorative rivets! *A bas* an eclectic aesthetic that recombines abstract expressionism, industrial symbolism, electric glow, and aesthitic excess into a revival of early Modernism—a style that is no less historical than that of the Renaissance! Is the Neomod of the beginning of the twenty-first century our Ecole des Beaux Arts—our equivalent of the revivalist style that twentieth-century Modernism explicitly reacted against? It was the ironical Henry Russell Hitchcock who wrote as early as 1936: "What we know as modern architecture has reached completion and is applicable as an academic discipline."[3]

Should not the modernism of our time engage the electronic digital technology appropriate for the current Information Age, rather than an ornamental industrial *rocaille* deriving from the historical Industrial Age? I once criticized architecture as frozen theory; now, how about architecture as bloated sculpture or minimalism cum electric glow for the Electronic Age? Seeing what is not effective is effective for understanding

11. Richard Rogers and Renzo Piano's Pompidou Center, Paris.

12. MeZZ popstage, Breda, Netherlands, by Erick van Egeraat associated architects (EEA).

13. Peter Zumthor's Kunsthaus Bregenz, Zurich, Switzerland.

what is effective. So here are two examples of what I consider the inappropriate kinds of architecture that dominate today—whose hype-expressionism needs, in musical terminology, *ma non troppo*.

Irony par excellence: the avant-garde architects of the early twentieth century could acknowledge and appreciate the American *industrial* vernacular architecture as relevant and could integrate it within an avant-garde architecture for the time—though admittedly it took those Central Europeans to do so. But the proclaimed avant-garde architects of the early twenty-first century cannot acknowledge and appreciate the American *commercial* vernacular architecture of their time as relevant and integrate it within a new architecture for their own time. Americans are snobbishly paranoid when it comes to an arguably vital everyday American architecture.

14. American commercial vernacular.

15. Interstate 95 near Philadelphia.

16, 17, 18. Las Vegas Strip, c. 1970.

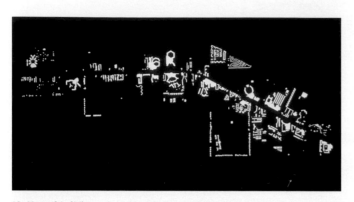

19. Map of buildings along the Las Vegas Strip, c. 1970 (from *Learning from Las Vegas*).

20. The Duck and the Decorated Shed (from *Learning from Las Vegas*).

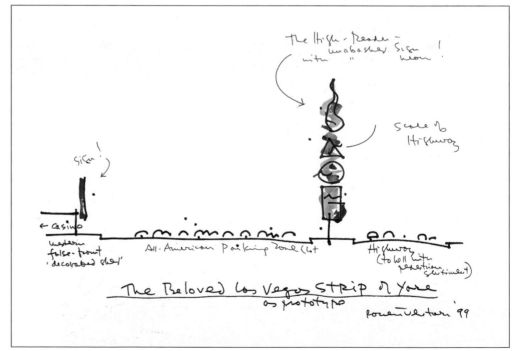

21. Robert Venturi's "The Beloved Las Vegas Strip of Yore."

22. Las Vegas, c. 2000.

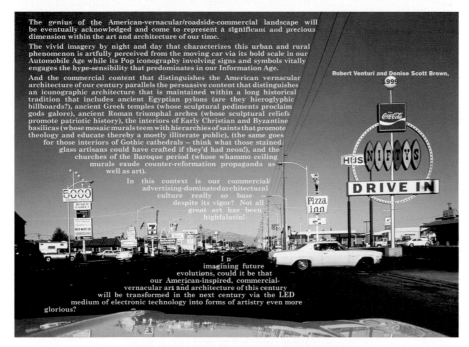

The genius of the American-vernacular/roadside-commercial landscape will be eventually acknowledged and come to represent a significant and precious dimension within the art and architecture of our time.

The vivid imagery by night and day that characterizes this urban and rural phenomenon is artfully perceived from the moving car via its bold scale in our Automobile Age while its Pop iconography involving signs and symbols vitally engages the hype-sensibility that predominates in our Information Age.

And the commercial content that distinguishes the American vernacular architecture of our century parallels the persuasive content that distinguishes an iconographic architecture that is maintained within a long historical tradition that includes ancient Egyptian pylons (are they hieroglyphic billboards?), ancient Greek temples (whose sculptural pediments proclaim gods galore), ancient Roman triumphal arches (whose sculptural reliefs promote patriotic history), the interiors of Early Christian and Byzantine basilicas (whose mosaic murals teem with hierarchies of saints that promote theology and educate thereby a mostly illiterate public), (the same goes for those interiors of Gothic cathedrals – think what those stained glass artisans could have crafted if they'd had neon!), and the churches of the Baroque period (whose whammo ceiling murals exude counter-reformation propaganda as well as art).

In this context is our commercial/advertising-dominated architectural culture really so base — despite its vigor? Not all great art has been highfalutin!

In imagining future evolutions, could it be that our American-inspired, commercial-vernacular art and architecture of this century will be transformed in the next century via the LED medium of electronic technology into forms of artistry even more glorious?

Robert Venturi and Denise Scott Brown, 1999

23. Interpretation of the classic Strip by Robert Venturi and Denise Scott Brown.

The following simple descriptions of precedents, valid as historical context, should help clarify the essential quality of architecture as sign or communication. Such precedents embrace essentially every period or style of architecture, engaging culture both high and low. They include:

- Ancient Egyptian architecture, with its temples and pylons whose surfaces are enveloped by hieroglyphics: are these not billboards for a proto-Information Age?

- Greek and Roman temples, whose pediments are ornamented with sculpture, swarming with gods and goddesses as expressive elements (as art) but also as symbolic elements (as iconography) for expounding the content of the religion the buildings accommodate, as indicated in one of the revival façades of the Philadelphia Museum of Art.

- The mosaic features lining and glorifying the naves of Early Christian churches in Ravenna, whose depicted sequences and hierarchies of saints we admire as works of art, and the grand conclusive nave in Cefalù—do not these architectural elements also explicitly instruct and educate a largely illiterate citizenry about Christian theology?

- And also the mosaic tesserae of Byzantine interiors and the stained glass windows essential to Gothic naves representing unequivocally supreme works of art—but are they not, through their varying kinds of glitter *and* their narrative content, also forms of propaganda as well as art? And think of what those stained glass artists could have accomplished for day *and* night if they had had neon!

- As for the fresco murals characteristic of the art of the Italian Renaissance and supreme as an element of the art of Western culture as a whole, they are convincingly described by the historian Marilyn Lavin in *The Place of Narrative* as originally an *explicit* element of narrative and an *incidental* work of art—the latter designation acquired via subsequent interpretation by historians of Western culture.[4] So here is quite explicitly communication as art rather than art as communication!

- And the vibrant murals integral to the ceilings of Baroque churches—are they not iconography as architecture, whose persuasive Counter-Reformation content is explicitly relevant to the interests of the Roman Catholic Church during that period of turmoil? *Stay a Catholic!* they seem to shout.
- The façade of a French Gothic cathedral with its statues of saints in niches depicted hierarchically: is this not a three-dimensional billboard in the center of town, covered with messages for the citizenry? Compare that with a modest vernacular row house turned into a church through a kind of iconographic layering.
- And what about the super-graphics lining the façades and terraces of Elizabethan manor houses as parapets *and* as kinds of static pre-electronic zippers?
- The *sgrafitto* patterns that adorn the exterior walls of Swiss chalets—do they not engage amenity and friendly scale within the natural context of a grand, and sometimes threatening, mountainous terrain?
- The Zen gardens of Kyoto—which represent/symbolize the natural landscape through diminution and stylization.
- And the PSFS building in Philadelphia, 1928–1932, perhaps the first high-rise Building in the International Style, which has always inspired me by its super-graphics that conform in scale to the city as a whole.
- And again remember Russian Constructivism, a form of Modernism that embraced iconography as integral within its formal compositions—and then Main Street, USA, perhaps a folk-art version of the same thing.
- And the American billboard as a commercial element ironically civic in its scale—why can't the modern billboard and the Modern building be integrated?
- But then, significantly and tragically, there is the example of Fascist architecture in Italy and Germany, whose simplified/abstract Classical surfaces abounded in graphic propaganda carved in stone.

24. Egyptian temple.

25. Philadelphia Museum of Art.

26. Byzantine Cathedral, Cefalù, Sicily.

27, 28. St. Apollinare Nuovo, Ravenna, Italy, and mosaic detail.

29. La Sainte Chapelle, Paris.

30. Cover, *The Place of Narrative*, by Marilyn Aronberg Lavin

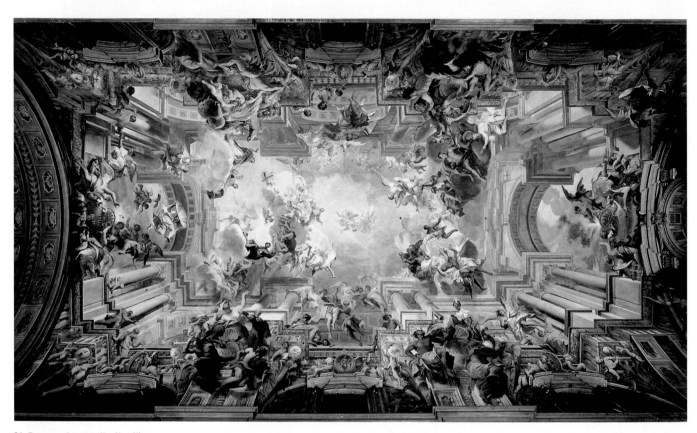

31. Baroque *trompe l'oeil* ceiling.

33. Cathedral, Amiens, France.

32. Row house church, Philadelphia.

34. John Dryden's Castle Ashby,
Northamptonshire, England.

35. Swiss chalet with sgraffito.

36. Japanese garden.

38. Main Street, U.S.A.

37. George Howe and William Lescaze's
PSFS Building, Philadelphia.

39, 40. Billboards with modern buildings.

We can acknowledge in the end that much art—except for the abstract art of the twentieth century—is incidental, is art secondarily. That is, its iconographic element dominates as a medium of description, explanation, persuasion. And is not this concept especially appropriate now for our Information Age, with its electronic technology? *Viva* electronic pixels as well as mosaic tesserae—as pixels ever-changing and evolving to accommodate multiculturalism! *Viva* iconography!

It has also been argued that the historical diminution of architectural iconography derived from the invention and influence of the printing press when the populace could read books and then also derived more recently from the invention and domination of the medium of television. But could it also be argued that the amount and dominance of information inherent for the Information Age can now increase the need for communication of all forms to acknowledge and accommodate the enhanced complexity of cultures?

VALID PRECEDENTS–RECENT AND CURRENT– FOR AN ARCHITECTURE AS SIGN

A valid architecture as sign for today derives mostly from America's automobile-driven commercial-vernacular precedent—as architecture for an Automobile Age, an Electronic Age, an Information Age—and engages Vernacular Loft architecture which is Conventional and Ordinary.

And for Denise and me it ultimately involves evolving—evolving from learning from Rome, engaging form and expression via *Complexity and Contradiction in Architecture*—to learning from Las Vegas, engaging symbolism and meaning via learning from *Learning from Las Vegas*—and then involving iconography and electronics that engage digital media as a significant element of architecture.

An architecture and urbanism that engages signage evolves from Main Street to the Strip to Route 95—where billboards serve as an equivalent of craft art today. While Main Street has evolved into a pedestrian mall—a polite version of Main Street, with its signage control, surrounded by barren parking areas—the essentially automobile-scale commercial strip is evolving into a Disneyland-like scenographic setting for commerce, as in the new Las Vegas. But now is the time for the electronic rather than for the scenographic!

Viva the loft and the generic/vernacular in a Mannerist Architecture as Communication!

It was Henry Russell Hitchcock who eloquently acknowledged the evolution of architecture beyond Modernism as early as 1936 and the relevance of ornament and a commercial vocabulary, and who wrote: "Great architecture . . . rises highest when it is based on a sound vernacular."[5] And Vincent Scully has referred to the valid "interaction between the vernacular and the classical traditions" in American historical architecture.[6]

41. Long Island's Big Duck, Flanders, New York.

One of the most vivid ideas to evolve from our Yale/Las Vegas Studio study of the quintessential strip was our distinction between the Duck and the Decorated Shed as architectural prototypes for our time: that is, the building as itself a symbol, exemplified by the Long Island Duck, a roadside stand we made famous (Peter Blake had first made it infamous) and that is now on the National Historical Register, and the building as generic loft whose aesthetic derives from its decorative or iconographic surfaces and/or applied signs. The Decorated Shed is the essential form of an Architecture as Communication, where meaning rather than expression is the quality sought, and where the aesthetic dimension derives from ornamental surface rather than from sculptural articulation.

42. Decorated Sheds, c. 1902.

It was Hitchcock who in 1936 again referred to each of these vernacular forms as relevant. Concerning the Duck: "Brown Derby roadside stands, and less abstruse symbolism of those which imitate at enormous scale ice-cream freezers or milk bottles, are an instance of the vernacular acceptance of an idea in America. The combination of strict functionalism and bold symbolism in the best roadside stands provides, perhaps, the most encouraging sign for the architecture of the mid-twentieth century."[7] Concerning the Decorated Shed he wrote, years before we did: "Ornament, but lately buried, is now in an embryonic

43. Sir Christopher Wren Building, College of William and Mary.

44. LeonBattista Alberti's Palazzo Rucellai, Florence.

45. Loft factory building, Philadelphia.

state preceding rebirth . . . free creative architecture . . . may well be distinguished by the quality of its applied ornament as much as by the originality of its composition."[8] And then there is J. B. Jackson, another precursor in the 1950s in his writings in his magazine *Landscape* on the significance of the American everyday/generic landscape.

So in the end it's *viva* the loft—as conventional and generic, as Decorated Shed for an Architecture as Sign, but the loft where the dumb and fanfare can be engaged!

***Viva* Form Accommodates Functions, rather than Form Follows Function!**
Architecture as generic/vernacular loft has a long and distinguished tradition of engaging a wide range of flexible internal programs. One can refer to the American mill or industrial loft, to the historical American academic building in the tradition of Princeton's Nassau Hall, Harvard's Massachusetts Hall, or the original hall at William and Mary by Sir Christopher Wren, as well as Sever Hall at Harvard by H. H. Richardson, which is my favorite building in America. And then there is the Italian palazzo spanning several centuries—Renaissance to Baroque—engaging over time a consistent spatial and formal system with varying stylistic façade surfaces; and the scientific research laboratory of today. All of these

kinds of buildings accommodate varied and evolving uses over time: the academic buildings housing classrooms, lecture halls, and dormitory spaces; the palazzi housing originally a dynastic family and then an embassy, consulate, library, or museum; and the laboratory being explicitly flexible as a loft for evolving spatial and mechanical-electronic configurations, or circulation inside that can enhance an element of community.

Here is architecture appropriate for our dynamic time, where form accommodates functions rather than form follows function, where form accommodates functions as a mitten rather than as a glove, to allow wiggle room for the varying fingers inside! And where the architectural quality derives from aesthetic patterns of surface—ornamental or iconographic—rather than from original sculptural articulation, as in the Richards Medical Research Laboratories at Penn, which is known for its functional/programmatic problems. *Viva* the mitten with wiggle room over the glove where form follows function!

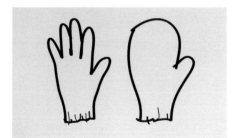

46. Louis Kahn's Richards Medical Research Laboratories, University of Pennsylvania.

47. VSBA's Gonda (Goldschmied) Neuroscience and Genetics Research Center, University of California, Los Angeles.

48. Glove vs. Mitten.

49. Unashamed generic orders.

Viva Conventional rather than Original for an Architecture as Communication!

The generic/vernacular architecture of the loft accommodates convention rather than promotes originality in its form and parallels thereby generic architecture in other forms that exemplify the great architecture of the past—the Classical temple, the Roman basilica (as law court and then, with the addition of transept, as Christian church), and the Italian palazzo with courtile. So here is valid architecture not only as conventional rather than original but as good rather than original—as the ideal. *A bas* "Ego-tecture"! *A bas* boring originality!

Viva Good rather than Original!

Michelangelo's dome with the drum for the crossing of St. Peter's is based on the same configuration created by Brunelleschi for the cathedral of Florence; it is therefore good rather than original—appropriate for our post-Romantic era where especially the architect as individual genius working in an ivory tower should be out and where art should embrace evolution as well as revolution in architecture.

Quotations from Douglas Kelbaugh's various letters, including some written to the editor of *The New York Times*, sum up the idea of good rather than original:

- "The twentieth-century binge on avant-garde, compulsive invention is starting to nauseate. History may remember the architects who want to be artists as the ones moving the proverbial deck chairs around on the *Titanic*. What appears now to be cutting edge or poetic may prove to be *fin de siècle* excess if not decadence."[9]
- "Change and audacity have become ends in and of themselves, as well as a prerequisite for media attention. Don't make excitement for its own sake habitual, mandatory or, worse yet, a style."[10]
- "There is now a rising interest in place. Witness the incredible number of recent books with the word 'place' in the title."[11]

50. Michelangelo's dome of St. Peter's, Rome. **51. Filippo Brunelleschi's Duomo, Florence.**

Or how about Vincent Scully's reference to "a liberation from the Romantic conception of the architect as the perennial inventor of the wheel. Modernism, and late Modernism in particular, was rent to incoherence by the insistence of its practitioners upon 'originality.'"[12]

Viva Ordinary rather than Extraordinary, or Ordinary made Extraordinary! And Ralph Waldo Emerson: "I embrace the common, I explore and sit at the feet of the familiar, the law. Give me insight into today, and you may have the antique and future worlds."[13] Acknowledge the ordinary, as in the Realist paintings of the nineteenth century, with landscape scenes of rural Provence and depictions of bohemian artists in cafés; as in the Pop Art of the twentieth century, with its depictions of commercial objects made special via modifications of medium, scale, and context.

52. Andy Warhol's *Campbell's Soup I.*

At our first submission to the Washington Fine Arts Commission many years ago, Gordon Bunshaft dismissed our design as ugly and

53. Surburban Main Street, U.S.A.

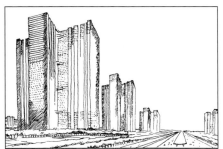

54, 55. Le Corbusier's Ville Radieuse.

ordinary. We took that as a compliment considering the source, and since then our motto has been "*Viva* Ugly and Ordinary!*A bas* Heroic and Original!" (You can buy caps with either of these mottos on them in the museum shop of the Philadelphia Museum of Art.

Viva Evolution rather than Revolution: the glory of the Everyday!

In architects' theories of planning in the twentieth century, the idea was to promote heroic utopia via revolution rather than accommodate pragmatic reality via evolution. Instead of acknowledging the possibilities of glory in the everyday, they gave us the mid-century Ville Radieuse, maintaining only bits of Paris. *A bas* Heroic! *Viva* Realism over Idealism! Dumb can be good!

Viva Learning from Las Vegas and Learning from *Learning from Las Vegas* for an Architecture of Communication

I refer to the historical (but still relevant) Strip era recorded by Denise, Steve, myself, and our Yale graduate students via verbal and graphic analysis and photographic images which worked to invigorate our projects as architects via learning from *Learning from Las Vegas*—and learning from Everything. *Viva* Realism! *A bas* Expressionism!

— 3 —
Architecture as Sign in the Work of VSBA

Here follows a series of projects of our firm, pre– and post–*Learning from Las Vegas*, that engage symbolism and ornament and emphasize iconographic content. This is not a review of our work in general but of a subset of design ideas, chronologically ordered, that engage especially graphic, symbolic, and sometimes electronic iconography, for an architecture as communication.

Given this focus, some of our otherwise significant planning studies and buildings are missing, as are frequently illustrations of interiors and references to function and program—all essential dimensions of design that are covered in Part II. Finally, many of the projects described here were never completed or were never built because they did not win a competition—but that is always the case with the practice of architecture.

Vanna Venturi House, Philadelphia, 1959–1964

A layered composition accommodating juxtapositions of contrasting exterior and interior forms. Its outer layer, as a sign on the front, symbolizes via silhouette and ornament an iconic house, with its sloping rather than flat roof and its conventional windows rather than absences of wall. Inner forms acknowledge the central chimney with integral stairwell and varying kinds of rooms. This complex building composition engages symbolism and mannerism inspired by the Villa Savoye, the Casa del Girasole, and the Low House, and not the Farnsworth House, which was the

56. Vanna Venturi House, Philadelphia.

characteristic house of the time. Maybe Mother's House should be known as Mannerist House.

Franklin Delano Roosevelt Memorial, competition project, 1960
A memorial in the form of an amenable promenade along the Potomac River in Washington, D.C. Its horizontal masonry surface evolves in section into a sloping vertical surface as a big-scale iconographic frieze along the side of the promenade, whose bas relief and graphics depict Roosevelt's life and significance. A continuous slot within this section works as an approach to and from a linear parking area beyond. Here is a proto–Vietnam Memorial at a civic scale engaging natural and urban context and symbolic content.

58, 59. Competition for FDR Memorial.

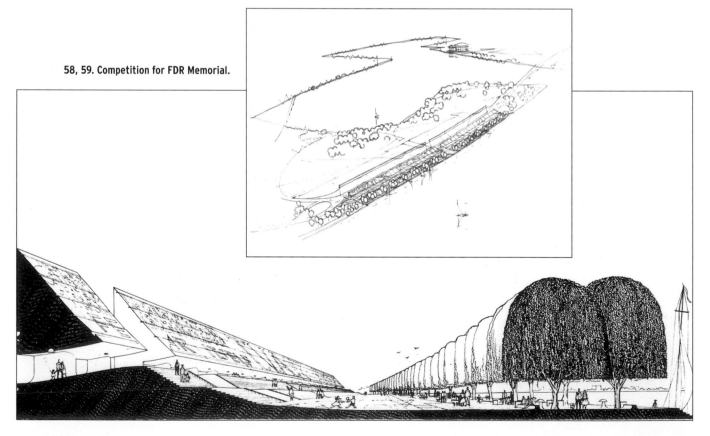

Grand's Restaurant, Philadelphia, 1961–1962

Renovation of an existing couple of row houses with shop windows on the ground floor. The interior design and furnishings are aesthetically conventional in the manner of a café, except for the big ornamental graphics on the walls. Upon the exterior façade, which we did not otherwise modify, is juxtaposed a sign, bold in size and scale and accommodating compositional duality and symbolic imagery, including the stylistic representation of a cup. It was removed in a few months at the demands of neighbors, who thought it vulgar! So here is a temporary combining of the ordinary/conventional with symbolism as fanfare—that became failure. But then twenty years later it reappeared at the entrance to the Whitney Museum on Madison Avenue—as revenge.

60. Grand's Restaurant, Philadelphia.

61. "High Styles" exhibition, Whitney Museum of Art, New York.

Guild House, Philadelphia, 1961–1966

Quaker housing for the elderly, which is not a concrete slab building in a park but a brick building along a street that accommodates to its ordinary urban context. The plan includes a maximum number of corner apartments with views. On the façade, ornamental elements and areas of pattern symbolize a base, a middle as a *piano nobile*, and an "attic," even though the actual layering of the floors inside is equal; the composition of the entrance forms a duality. There was originally a TV antenna on top symbolizing entertainment for the elderly, and there still is a big sign over the entrance at the scale of the wide street it faces and integral within the composition. The windows are unashamedly conventional—holes in walls rather than absences of walls. All of these ordinary elements were extraordinary in the early 1960s. And it really took courage to apply the ornamental white stripe on the façade—at the time I was asking myself, "Am I a pervert?" We have just learned that the building is now on the Philadelphia Register of Historical Places, even though the architect is still alive!"

62. Guild House, Philadelphia.

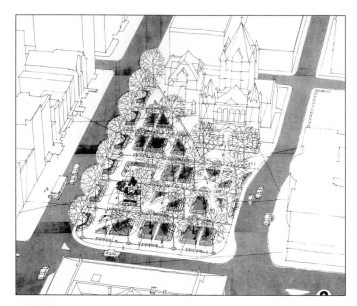

63. Competition for Copley Square, Boston.

64. Fire Station #4, Columbus, Indiana.

Copley Square, Boston, Massachusetts, competition, 1965–1966

An iconographic redesign for the existing plaza in front of H. H. Richardson's Trinity Church. The conventional American urban street system is represented in miniature, the blocks are amenably raised 18 inches along the edges so that people can sit, and a civic statue as a building represents the great/beloved church.

Fire Station No. 4, Columbus, Indiana, 1966–1968

Here is a sign on a civic building that is integral architecturally, big and not carved in stone, and with pattern on its brick façade to enhance the architectural expression. The client accepted shocking signage and pattern in 1966 and continues to take good care of it.

The Football Hall of Fame, competition entry, 1967

Here is what we call a "bill-ding-board"—an example of architecture as communication par excellence—the integration of sign and building, where from a parking lot on a Saturday afternoon you can sit in your car or have a picnic and watch moving imagery on the bill-

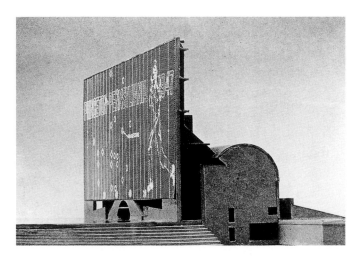

board as information and entertainment. But the architecture of this building is also up to some mannerist mischief: its interior behind the billboard consists of a basilican nave of a generic Christian church but bordered only on one side with niches as chapels—a design acknowledging the description of the building's program in the competition literature as virtually a sports sanctuary memorializing athletes as saints. Upon the vaulted ceiling of the nave is a movie screen as a mural or as a digitally-animated screen consisting of Baroque/Tiepolo-like floating athletes as saints truly moving via new technology. The chapel-like niches along one side of the nave contain relics including perhaps once-smelly sweatshirts rather than body parts of saintly individual football players.

Thousand Oaks City Hall and Civic Center, California, 1969

A design for a competition we did not win: a civic building, ordinary as a two-story linear loft, to accommodate changing governmental departments of a changing city over time, but also like a series of commercial shops, each with a sign on the front indicating the particular department it houses. The building faces a convenient parking area which is part of

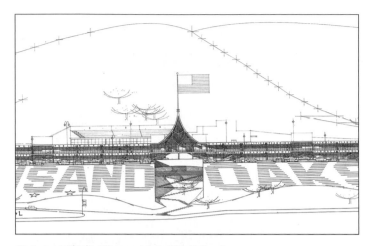

67. Competition for Thousand Oaks City Hall and Convention Center.

the architectural composition in the manner of a highway commercial mall. What is extraordinary is the huge signage extending the length of the complex on a berm in front of the building, to be seen from U.S. Route 101. The central part of the building, via the configuration of its structural framing, depicts an oak leaf and supports the biggest flag in the nation! All of the above composition works to accommodate context, as this is a civic building in southern California, to be seen from a car moving along Route 101.

The Exhibition on Venturi and Rauch, Whitney Museum of Art, New York City, 1971

A free-standing, two-sided, back-lit "billboard" teeming with small-scale information to be seen close-up.

International Bicentennial Exposition Master Plan project, 1971–1972

A design for the proposed Philadelphia World's Fair of 1976—the complex as a Way of Signs inspired by the classic American highway along which a variety of things can happen. There are all kinds of individualistic pavilions and exhibitions, yet a sense of the whole is maintained at the same time through the inherent, consistent continuity of the "highway" itself. This continuity as foil to the variety of incidents along the way is reinforced by the consistent series of overhead signs—like the conventional green signs spanning interstate highways that clarify directions and create identity. Here they emit general information as communication to maintain a sense of the whole within the parts and also act as elements of fanfare. The approaches to the site along existing streets and highways are bordered by billboards illustrating examples of Philadelphian culture, high and low—like Poussin at the Philadelphia Museum of Art and Philly cheesesteaks in South Philadelphia.

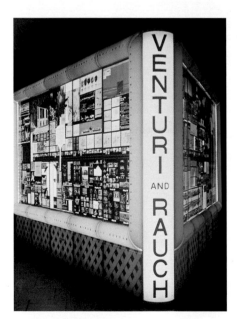

68. Exhibition on Venturi and Rauch, Whitney Museum of Art, New York.

69. International Bicentennial Exposition Master Plan project.

70. "City Edges" study.

Addition to the Allen Memorial Art Museum, Oberlin College, 1973–1977
Our first academic building, awarded us by the then director, Richard Spear, where we could immediately attach a generic gallery space to a distinguished Beaux Arts–style building of the second decade of the twentieth century. Inside, there is external lighting from above, deriving from a series of clerestory windows and modulated by hanging translucent plastic panels. A separate wing houses an art library and conservation laboratory, as a recessive generic loft in an ordinary style of the time. But the new main gallery on the outside in the front could be adorned with an explicitly decorative all-over pattern in the materials of the original building, achieving harmony between the old and the new through contrast and analogy. But the main thing is this: decorative pattern at that

71. Addition to the Allen Memorial Art Museum, Oberlin College.

72. "Ironic column," addition to the Allen Memorial Art Museum, Oberlin College.

73. Sign for the Whitney Museum of Art, New York.

time was unheard of, and attaching the new directly to the old without a transition was also hard to do—if valid. And then there was the Ironic (rather than Ionic) column in the rear—the first example of historical reference in architecture in the last half of the century.

Signs for the Whitney Museum of Art, New York City, 1974–1976 and 1984–1985

Two signs atop the *porte cochère* announce and identify two different exhibitions, and read effectively (through scale and symbolism) within the context of Marcel Breuer's Whitney Museum and upper Madison Avenue. (See also Figure 61.)

Eclectic houses, 1977

A series of identical pavilions but with varying flat front elevations, each playfully engaging stylistic symbolism of all kinds. The Doric Temple was constructed in a Maine landscape in 2002.

75. "Doric Temple" shed, Mount Desert Island, Maine.

74. Eclectic Houses.

76. BASCO Showroom, Philadelphia.

77. MoMA Queens, Long Island City, New York.

BASCO Showroom and Warehouse, Philadelphia, 1976

An existing loft building along a highway, converted to a retail show-room/outlet and to architecture as communication—here, commercial communication. We painted its façade dark blue and ornamented it with super-graphics: five bright-red free-standing three-dimensional sculptural letters about 40 feet high forming a layer in front (alas, now demolished). A quarter of a century later, a civic building—the MOMA Queens satellite museum—expresses a similar form of communication. We were never Postmodern, but maybe we are pre-Modern?

The ISI building in Philadelphia, 1977–1979, and the BEST Products Showroom in Bucks County, Pennsylvania, 1973–1979

Both are conventional generic lofts as decorated sheds. The former is an office headquarters with a main façade as a pixilated punch card in brick and colored tiles which might symbolize the digital era work going on inside, and an entrance which, in contrast, is ornamented with a flowered pattern and big graphics. The latter is a storage/showroom whose porcelain-enameled panel façades are ornamented with pretty flower patterns and graphics whose scale is big enough to be read from a highway, yet are in the context of a parking lot. This design became known as the biggest shower curtain in Bucks County!

78. Institute for Scientific Information, Philadelphia.

79. BEST Showroom, Oxford Valley, Pennsylvania.

Knoll Furniture, 1978–1984

A series of chair designs inspired by those of Charles and Ray Eames, who also used a product of modern technology, bent plywood. Yet the stylistic references in the design of these chairs contributes an aesthetic dimension not permissible within pure Modernism—a representational/symbolic/historical reference via silhouette that is not literal. And then there are the various patterns when the surfaces are plastic rather than wood.

80. Knoll Furniture, Knoll Showroom, New York.

The Coxe-Hayden House and Studio, Block Island, Rhode Island, 1979–1980

A mannerist version of houses small in size but big in scale, representing and symbolizing the New England Shingle Style house as shelter, but not reviving the style as such. These buildings are similar to the two Trubek-Wislocki Houses of Nantucket of 1970–1972 that recall, via their setting, the Greek temples by the sea at Selinunte, Sicily, despite the mannerist exceptions within their compositions.

81. Coxe-Hayden House and Studio, Block Island, Rhode Island.

Gordon Wu Hall, Princeton University, 1980–1983

A brick dining hall situated and designed to identify the center of Butler College, made up of existing dormitories all in brick. The entrance enhances the identity of this otherwise recessive building through the bold symbolic pattern adorning it, which refers to Elizabethan/Jacobean motifs often found over fireplaces and appropriate within the context of a quasi–Elizabethan-style precinct of the campus.

82. Gordon Wu Hall, Princeton University.

83. Iconic design for Times Square Development project.

84, 85. Clinical Research Building, University of Pennsylvania.

Iconic design for Times Square Development project, New York City, 1984
At the request of a developer, an element to sit within Philip Johnson's then-current Postmodernist design for a tasteful Times Square—an icon as identifiable and memorable for New York City as the Statue of Liberty.

Clinical Research Building, University of Pennsylvania, Philadelphia, 1985–1989
A science laboratory as a generic loft to accommodate spatial, mechanical, and electronic flexibility. The interior plan makes exceptions for "light at the end of the corridor" and niches for incidental meetings and communication among users. Exterior form and surfaces create rhythmic consistency, and occasional exceptions—slight articulations of the ends of the building, louvers for mechanical units at the top, and explicit ornamental brick patterns on the façade—create aesthetic tension. And then there are the iconographic seals of the University at the scale of, and identifiable from, the region, via their size, height, and bold colors. For this almost rural campus, the design works up close and from the commercial urban context beyond. Here is exterior fanfare, which is more appropriate than interior fanfare, now popular, which would consist of a spatial atrium.

The Sainsbury Wing of the National Gallery, London, England, 1985–1991
A building that may be looked at as essentially a loft building in the tradition of the palatial art museum—but with some specific reference to Sir John Soane's Dulwich Picture Gallery. The front façade as sign is independent of the other three façades of the wing, as it acknowledges its context: the original historical building, which it is a continuation of, and Trafalgar Square, which it faces.

86. Sainsbury Wing, National Gallery, London.

This façade as billboard relates to the façade of the original building through analogy and contrast—that is, its Classical elements are exact replications of those of the original façade, but their positions relative to one another vary significantly to create compositional inflection of the new façade toward the old façade, while at the same time maintaining a unified monumental face toward the grand square. And the important element of rhythm varies significantly from the old façade to the new: the spacing of the exactly replicated architectural elements of the new façade (the pilasters, and so on) is jazzy—a counterpoint to that of the old façade, whose spacing might suggest the rhythm of a minuet or a gavotte. Here is a building in its context that is not historical-revival, not Postmodern, not Neomodern. It is an urban mannerist billboard!

Philadelphia Orchestra Hall project, 1987–1996

A building designed at the specific request of the client to accommodate the modest budget of a Quaker meeting house rather than the grand budget of a Baroque opera house. It is designed as a building that also accommodates to its specific urban setting, South Broad Street, which is

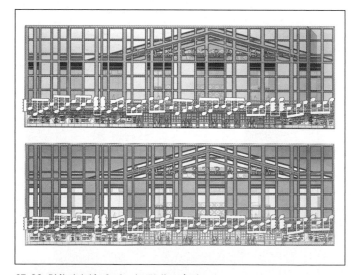

87, 88. Philadelphia Orchestra Hall project.

ELEVATION
UNITED STATES PAVILION - EXPO '92
SEVILLE SPAIN
VENTURI RAUCH AND SCOTT BROWN
APRIL 1989

identified through varied kinds of buildings that sit consistently along it rather than back from it—whether major or minor, commercial or civic, in the Philadelphian/American tradition. (Even if this were a grand American opera house, it could not sit at the end of an axial Avenue de l'Opéra!) Its main façade along Broad Street is designed therefore to be seen obliquely and from eye-level; it also is colorful in the tradition of the façades of other civic buildings in Philadelphia, such as the Pennsylvania Academy of the Fine Arts and the Philadelphia Museum of Art.

And very important, its symbolism and iconography are rich—its rhythmically complex and dissonant curtain wall can be read ambiguously by day as conventional/modular-Modern and ambiguously by night through the use of spandrel glass panels as representative of a pedimented Classical façade with pilasters. At its base and at eye level are digitized moving message boards to inform pedestrians about changing cultural events in the community, and above is a decorative, three-dimensional floating frieze in metal, representing the notes of the right hand's opening bars in the third movement of the "Moonlight Sonata." Inside the hall is a hall for symphonic music ornamented with symbolic windows and not a theatric opera house cum stage that separates the audience from the orchestra.

Competition entry for the United States Pavilion for Expo '92, Seville, Spain, 1989

An appropriately huge generic loft to accommodate varieties of uses, spaces, effects inside and to read effectively outside from the front via a monumental billboard façade engaging unforgettable iconic communication rather than articulations as abstract form. Our design also accommodated the building's low construction budget; the winning scheme, which was articulated/sculptural, eventually could not be built within the budget.

90. Children's Museum of Houston, Texas.

Children's Museum of Houston, Texas, 1989–1992

A low-budget building employing functional generic prefabricated Butler buildings to accommodate flexibility for the major exhibition space. The explicitly ornamental/symbolic façade on the front features a child's interpretation of a classic Classical art museum for adults. The side where school buses arrive is faced with a long *porte cochère* supported by a series of what we call caryakids. The building was built within the budget and is popular.

91. Stevenson Library, Bard College.

Stevenson Library, Bard College, 1989–1993

A flexible loft whose front façade is identified by its vivid colors as the main entrance of the complex almost hidden around a corner. The rhythmic composition relates to that of the Classical façade of the original building to which it is attached, and to the entrance pavilion which responds symbolically to the same historical façade.

Hôtel du Département de la Haute-Garônne, Toulouse, France, 1990–1999

A complex as a provincial capitol within the beautiful urban context of a city whose rose aura derives from its predominantly brick buildings. This building serves essentially as an office complex consisting of two generic slab buildings whose consequent rhythmic consistency is programmatically and aesthetically interrupted by exceptions—the grand legislative hall and the governor's (M. le Président's) elaborate office complex and other spe-

92. Hôtel du Département de la Haute-Garônne, Toulouse, France.

93. Historic columns, Toulouse, France.

cial elements. The consequent essential linearities of the building-forms in plan permit the building to create an exterior way that is arcaded, and thereby to fit into and become part of the urban texture of the setting.

The symbolic elements that accommodate the urban context and acknowledge the civic program consist of: the façades as brick with sandstone patterns; the two-dimensional representations of monumental columns that introduce the main entrance to the way and refer to, and represent, a pair of historical columns that originally adorned the site as an entrance to the city; the rainbow pattern on the glass façade of the legislative hall referring to the iconic symbol of the province; faux windows on the interior walls of the hall, with representations of Magritte-like clouds on a wall behind, which work to make the space read as a symbolic civic hall as well as a functional auditorium; and patterns as abstractions of architectural ornament on the façades of historical buildings typical of the old city.

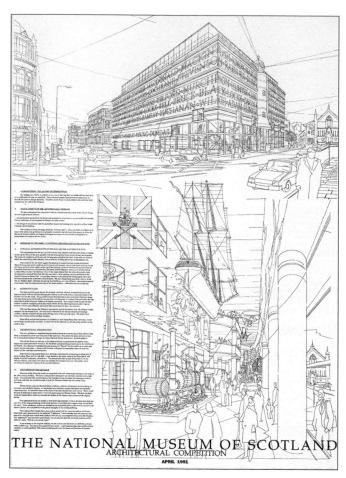

THE NATIONAL MUSEUM OF SCOTLAND
ARCHITECTURAL COMPETITION
APRIL 1991

94. Competition for the National Museum of Scotland.

Significant exceptions to the elements described above are the sandstone façades of the exterior of the complex, which contrast with the red brick façades of the interior way of the complex and thereby enhance their effect within the whole, and the glass façades of the two pedestrian covered bridges that cross over the way. So here is a building of its time in a distinguished historical city that acknowledges the validity and power of symbolic forms and patterns as well as abstract forms in a particular context.

Museum of Scotland, Edinburgh, 1991

A submission for a building competition that essentially disallowed windows on the façades. Therefore we ornamented the building with the names of great scientists inscribed in the masonry—architecture as information whose precedents are the façades of Henri Labroust's Bibliothèque Ste. Geneviève, which teems with the names of cultural figures, and Egyptian hieroglyphic surfaces of long ago?

Loker Commons in Harvard University's nineteenth-century Gothic Revival Memorial Hall, 1992–1996

A student center in a kind of Romantic basement, conceived as an appropriate place for students to hang out. The aesthetic is that of a teenager's bedroom, where the architect's intrusion is apparently minimal. The two main architectural elements are electronic-iconographic—that is, a four-color LED video panel at the end of a way through the main space that can also be watched obliquely from a nearby café space, and a three-color LED zipper frieze along the main buffet counter, displaying linear moving messages. A series of big old-fashioned bulletin tack-boards completes the variety of media that make this essentially a center of community and communication within the institution. One problem, it turned out, was that the organization for maintaining a dynamic electronic communication system was hard to establish and maintain at the university.

Trabant Student Center, University of Delaware, Newark, 1992–1996
A campus community building whose main component is an interior way at the scale of the exterior campus as a whole and whose spatial direction corresponds to, and works as, a segment of an important pedestrian path of the campus as a whole. So as a way as well as a place it encourages specific and incidental meetings among students, and as a communal/communicative place it is highly populated. Along one side of the way, bordered with chairs and tables, are windows connecting inside and outside; and on the other side are big niches containing shops crowded with commercial signs, including those of McDonald's, Taco Bell, and so on, and beyond them are spaces for specific campus activities and organizations. The architectural way is ornamented on the ceiling with neon tubes as arches which spatially reinforce and celebrate this continuous way along a way. And the neon on the signs vividly engages everyday commercial convention as an element within a rural campus.

The Whitehall Ferry Terminal for Lower Manhattan, 1992–1996
A building to accommodate its immediate program and to work as a civic monument within its urban context as perceived from the north and within its natural context as approached from the south, against the skyline of lower Manhattan as approached by ferry from across the bay. Against the background of high-rises as seen from the south, this important civic building is tiny, and its relative importance must derive from its big/civic-scale, electronic brilliance and symbolic/iconographic content. It is significant therefore that the private buildings (the high-rises) behind are big in size but small in scale, while the civic building up front is small in size but big in scale.

Design No. 1 presents the façade as a grand sign with a digital-electronic surface depicting a clock-face—an appropriate symbolic element

95. Loker Commons, Memorial Hall, Harvard University.

96. Trabant Student Center, University of Delaware.

97, 98. Whitehall Ferry Terminal project, New York.

that was explicitly decorative, now that clocks are virtually obsolete at transportation centers because everyone has a watch. The otherwise generic building behind has a vaulted roof approximately corresponding to the curve of the upper part of the clock.

Design No. 2 accommodates a later reduction in the budget and consists of a building as pure loft whose façade toward the bay includes a big parapet as a blatant sign depicting a fragment of an American flag, whose stripes wave via digital movement. Upon the sign can also be juxtaposed moving graphics that emit information, civic and otherwise. The partly curving profile of the parapet echoes the round profile of the former clock as an element that is in contrast to the orthogonal compositions of the skyscrapers beyond. Here is architecture of communication iconically imageful for lower Manhattan—a twenty-first-century counterpoint to the nineteenth-century Statue of Liberty seen to the left and whose technology and aesthetic are appropriately not industrial/sculptural but electronic/iconographic.

Mielparque Nikko Kirifuri Resort Hotel and Spa, Nikko, Japan, 1992–1997
A building complex in a national forest. From the outside it is a series of

100, 101. Spa, Mielparque Nikko Kirifuri Resort Hotel and Spa, Nikko, Japan.

modern buildings with flat roofs, but applied ornamental aluminum beams represent those of traditional sloped roofs and, when perceived obliquely, create the effect of solid overhangs. Ornamental patterns on the end façades represent the frame structure of traditional façades and the composition of Mondrian paintings. The pattern of the end façade of the indoor tennis building depicts Mondrian's *Broadway Boogie-Woogie*. So here are functional conventional buildings of our time adorned via symbolic elements.

Inside, the hotel lobby works as a stylization of a Japanese village street, whose everyday elements—green public telephones, ornamental fake flowers, dispensing machines, and signs galore—are represented two-dimensionally at an exaggerated scale, as in Pop Art paintings. The great hall of the indoor swimming pool is adorned above by aluminum panels as representations of huge leaves suspended from structural trusses that face swimmers as they glide up and down the pool—spring-like green on one side and autumn-like yellow on the other side. So here is conventional Modern architecture which communicates via varied elements applied as signage. A gracious quotation from our friend Akio Izutsu: "[This hotel] is loved by visitor[s] because . . . it lets them feel human warmth."

99. "Village Street," Mielparque Nikko Kirifuri Resort Hotel and Spa, Nikko, Japan.

102. Competition for office tower in New York City.

Competition for office tower, 43rd Street and Eighth Avenue, New York City, 1994

A high-rise whose lower façade engages architecture as sign, whose main shaft works as a loft-like tower, and whose top becomes an explicit element of fanfare to be seen from a distance.

Perelman Quad, University of Pennsylvania, Philadelphia, 1994–2000

A central outdoor space for the campus as a whole—known as Wynn Commons—identifies this student center as a precinct rather than a building. It is defined implicitly by existing bordering buildings with varied architectural styles and façade materials but defined explicitly via pylons identifying the four main entrances to the space. The surfaces of the pylons are covered with graphic information, including history lessons concerning the institution. (Alas, we were required to diminish the height of the pylons as originally designed to accommodate "good taste.") And the great shield above a platform at the eastern end is explicitly a sign which works to terminate one end of the space and give it identity—and contribute sparkle—via explicit symbolism/iconography. Inside Houston Hall above the central information desk is an LED board with ever-changing community information.

103. Wynn Commons, Perelman Quadrangle, University of Pennsylvania.

U.S. Embassy for Berlin competition project, 1995

A building as loft in the tradition of a palace to accommodate flexible programmatic space inside and security needs. It was also designed to work as a recessive form within the context of the Brandenberg Gate and the Pariser Platz, but whose appropriate iconographic fanfare within its entry courtyard can be glimpsed from the Platz in the form of permanent graphics carved in stone and of electronic LED media—another kind of mural whose active content emits cultural and communal information.

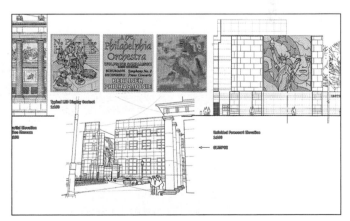

104, 105. Competition for U.S. Embassy in Berlin.

Trenton Central Fire Headquarters and Museum, New Jersey, 1995–2001
A firehouse fitting into an old brick neighborhood but sitting comfortably also, via its integral graphics on its façade, into a city famous for its huge civic sign spanning the Delaware River on a bridge— TRENTON MAKES, THE WORLD TAKES—which I have loved since I was a child.

106. Trenton Central Fire Headquarters and Museum, Trenton, New Jersey.

McDonald's, Lake Buena Vista, Florida, 1996–1998

A classic example of American commercial architecture defined by signage and symbolism within a roadside context whose conventional order we tweaked, in cooperation with McDonald's.

107. McDonald's, Lake Buena Vista, Florida.

108, 109. Frist Campus Center, Princeton University.

Frist Campus Center, Princeton University, 1996–2000

A community center combining a renovation of the former Palmer Physics Building in a Jacobean style with a new addition that engages communication through spatial circulation and iconography involving several kinds of media. Outside, a layer as a kind of two-dimensional arcade in front of the historical Palmer façade creates a symbolically multi-entranced community building. Its graphic frieze had to be modified to pass a local ordinance that minimized vulgarity: we made the "sign" ambiguous and therefore mannerist! On the other side of the complex is a new façade applied as a layered curtain wall whose glass surface contains a fritted pattern to conserve energy—a pattern very big in its scale but subtle in its effect depicting a Princeton shield visible inside and out and working also to distinguish this structure as a community building relating to the whole campus. Inside along its circulation/streets and elsewhere are neon signs at a café and a bar, stylized verbal graffiti painted on the old brick bearing walls of the Palmer-side basement as quotations from famous Princetonians, and, in front of a café along one of the interior ways, a rear-projection video wall, whose operation has been beautifully organized to announce campus activities as well as to project slides from current art history courses.

Extension of the football stadium at its outer perimeter, University of Michigan, 1997–1998

Intended to return the stadium to the status of the biggest among the Big Ten. We also added a maize and blue "halo" as a decorative metal parapet adorned

110, 111. Extension of Michigan Stadium.

with symbols and words at the edge of our outer extension of six rows of benches. But this iconographic dimension offended the sports fans of the institution (although they attend games wearing clothes and carrying accessories graphically emblazoned with Michigan logos, not to mention inscribing their own bodies!); the iconography had to be removed after two seasons.

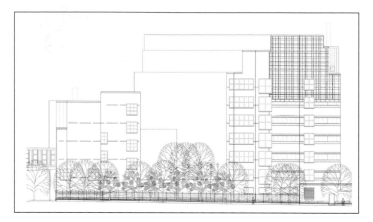

**Anlyan Center for Medical Research and Education,
Yale University School of Medicine, 1998–2003**
An enormous architectural complex consisting of
flexible lofts. The apparent size and scale is perceptually diminished on the exterior by wall surface patterns in a variety of materials and by an
iconographic decorative/sculptural element as fanfare depicting a row of trees on the rear façade
which turns a friendly face toward the local town
and softens the effect of the security fencing.

Chicago Crown Fountain project, 2000
A fountain as a representation—as a metal sign-board engaging the
technology of LED whose surface, containing colorful moving patterns
of pixels, works effectively within its bold and rich urban context at the
edge of Lake Michigan and appropriately for today.

**The California NanoSystems Institute, University of California, Santa
    Barbara, 2001–present**
A façade as communication—via a pixilated electronic medium especially appropriate for this context. The east elevation of the complex
faces the main entrance to the university, which is vehicle-frequented
rather than pedestrian-frequented. A part of this elevation requiring no
windows becomes a 45×45 foot screen—integral to the whole façade,
and at a scale and brilliance appropriate as it is perceived from moving
vehicles entering the campus. The changing content on the screen
ranges from announcements about the Media Arts and Technology
Program to notices about the Active Digital Media Program of the Art
Department to university-wide information. This architecture as communication can also work as an iconic element to identify the institution
as a whole. Alas, the LED screen of the UCSB project was rejected by
the Regents and so cannot go ahead as an example of architecture as
sign—which is why we have to lecture and write books.

114. The California NanoSystems Institute, University of California at Santa Barbara.

Lehigh Valley Hospital, Muhlenberg, Bethlehem, Pennsylvania, 2002–present
The front façade represents, appropriately, a friendly red-brick loft building whose frame structure is expressed via aluminum appliqué. A two-dimensional arcade in limestone with an ornamental blue H works as an icon to identify the hospital from afar and close-up. Another bigger H as sculpture is located along the highway to further identify the institution via iconography.

115. Lehigh Valley Hospital-Muhlenberg, Bethlehem, Pennsylvania.

Penn's Landing Development Plan, Philadelphia, 2003

A civic place along the Delaware River whose composition is layered, with big BASCO-like letters spelling CAMDEN along a river promenade, beyond which is a civic space, and then an electronic billboard beyond that, whose content would be ornamental and informational. The billboard also could be free-standing or could be the façade of a building—as a parking garage and/or residential high-rise with civic and commercial uses on the ground level. And beyond that layer, varied private development could evolve over time as appropriate for the developer. Across the river from Philadelphia are letters spelling PHILADELPHIA to perceptually and symbolically connect the two cities, each now vividly apparent from either side of the river. Here is civic composition with iconic effect.

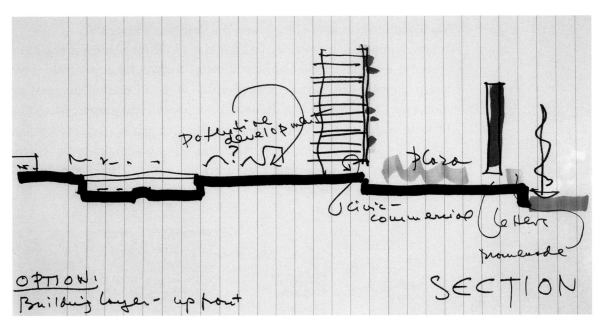

OPTION:
Building layer – up front

potential development?

plaza

civic-commercial

letter

promenade

SECTION

116, 117, 118. Penn's Landing Development Plan project, Philadelphia.

Two high-rise/skyscraper office towers for Shanghai, China, 2003

At last an opportunity to design a high-rise—and for Shanghai, the multicultural city par excellence of yesterday, today, and tomorrow! This design engages the surface iconography of LED media, juxtaposing upon a generic loft building decorative, symbolic, and graphic images at different scales—some static, others changing. Each is a loft *and* a tower *and* a billboard accommodating hype-sensibility where dramatic fanfare derives from surface-pixilated iconography rather than from formal articulated expressionism!

119, 120, 121. Project for High-Rise/Skyscraper-Office Towers, Shanghai, China.

— 4 —
A New Mannerism, for Architecture as Sign

So here is complexity and contradiction as mannerism, or mannerism as the complexity and contradiction of today—in either case, today it's mannerism, not Modernism.

At the beginning of the twentieth century, an aesthetic revolution made sense via a Modern architecture that was a stylistic adaptation of a current vernacular/industrial way of building—just as in the mid-fifteenth century an aesthetic revolution made sense via a Renaissance architecture that was a stylistic revival of an ancient vocabulary, that of Roman architecture. At the same time, in the Modernist style an industrial vocabulary was paradoxically accommodated within an abstract aesthetic, just as in the Renaissance style a pagan/Classical vocabulary was paradoxically accommodated within an explicitly Christian culture. And can it now be said that an aesthetic evolution makes sense at the beginning of the twenty-first century, engaging a mannerist architecture evolved from the preceeding style, that of classic Modernism—just as an aesthetic evolution made sense in the mid-sixteenth century engaging a mannerist architecture evolved from the preceeding style, that of High Renaissance?

In *Complexity and Contradiction in Architecture* I referred to

> a complex architecture, with its attendant contradictions, [as] not only a reaction to the banality or prettiness of current architecture. It [can also represent an] attitude common in . . . mannerist periods [and can also be] a continuous strain among diverse architects [in history]. Today this attitude is again relevant to both the medium of architecture and the program in architecture. First, the medium of architecture must be re-examined if the increased scope of our architecture as well as the complexity of its goals is to be expressed. Simplified forms or superficially complex forms will not work. Instead, the variety inherent in the ambiguity of visual perception must once more be

acknowledged and exploited. Second, the growing complexities of our functional programs must be acknowledged.[1]

In that work, I described, through comparative analysis, historical examples of mannerist architecture, explicit and implicit, that acknowledge complexity and contradiction in their composition, but I did not prescribe a resultant architecture for the time. This lack of prescription was noted by Alan Chimacoff and Alan Plattus as positive in their essay in *The Architectural Record* of September 1983.[2] But here and now, through a reconsideration of complexity and contradiction as it currently evolves, I wish to prescribe a specific direction, if not a style—that of Architecture as Sign—and describe a specific manner, that of mannerism, explicitly appropriate for our time. I shall rely again here on analyses of historical examples of mannerist architecture and urbanism—plus one example of our own work—to verify and clarify the evolutionary idea of mannerism and the complexity and contradiction it inherently embraces.

WHAT IS MANNERISM?

Mannerism—not discovered or acknowledged as a style until the mid-nineteenth century—is, according to Nikolaus Pevsner, "indeed full of mannerisms."[3] And it is by definition hard to define: Arnold Hauser has written, "It can be rightly complained that there is no such thing as a clear and exhaustive definition of mannerism."[4] Is not that an appropriate acknowledgment for our own era—exemplified by multiculturalism and by technologies evolving by leaps and bounds? But here is my attempt at a definition of mannerism in architecture appropriate for now:

> Mannerism as Convention Tweaked—or as Modified Convention Acknowledging Ambiguity. Mannerism for architecture of our time that acknowledges conventional order rather than original expression but breaks the conventional order to accommodate complexity and contradiction and thereby engages ambiguity—engages ambiguity unambiguously. Mannerism as complexity and contradiction applied to convention—as acknowledging a conventional order that is then modified or broken to accommodate valid exceptions and

acknowledge unambiguous ambiguities for an evolving era of complexity and contradiction—rather than acknowledging no order or acknowledging a totality of exceptions or acknowledging a new order so as to be original.

These characteristics are what can distinguish a mannerist approach appropriate for today from a Neomodernist approach, which abhors convention as ordinary and adores originality as anything to be different.

So convention, system, order, genericness, *manners* must be there in the first place before they can be broken—think of the British aristocracy's tendency to break the rules of etiquette in order to imply confidence about knowing them so well and therefore ease in not following them consistently. Later I shall describe what I consider a parallel mannerist trend in British architecture throughout its history.

It is certainly significant that the most vivid manifestation of mannerism occurs immediately after the High Renaissance, where convention as a style was most explicit and therefore most vividly breakable. So here is a definition of mannerism where convention is inherent but at times given up on and made thereby exceptionally unconventional—a definition that does not involve originality or revolution, which is for our time a bore. Here is a list of elements of a mannerist architecture that acknowledges and accommodates the complexity and contradiction of today (appropriately, in no order except alphabetical):

Accommodation
Ambiguity
Boredom
Both-and
Breaks
Chaos
Complexity
Contradiction
Contrast
Convention broken
Deviations

Difficult whole
Discontinuity
Disorder
Dissonance
Distortion
Diversity
Dualities
Dumbness
Eclectic
Everyday
Exceptions
Generic broken
Imbalance
Inconsistency
Incorrect
Inflection
Irony
Jumps in scale
Juxtapositions
Layering
Meaning
Monotony
Naïveté
Obscurity
Ordinary
Paradox
Pluralism
Pop
Pragmatism
Reality
Scales (plural)
Sophistication
Syncopation
Tension

Terribilitá
Vernacular
Wit
Wrestling

I refer here not to the total inconsistency of recent Decon architecture, for example, which ends up as total consistency, and not to the *dramatique* inconsistency of current Neomodern architecture, for example, which ends up as abstract sculpture. So here is a further list of notes concerning what mannerism is *not:*

Contorted
Excessive
Ideological
Mannered
Minimalist
Picturesque
Polite
Willful

There are two kinds of mannerism in architecture that can be acknowledged: Explicit and Implicit. Explicit might refer to the particular style of a particular period, that of the mid-sixteenth century in Italy in its purest and predominant form—to the extent mannerism can be pure—and spelled therefore with a capital M. Implicit mannerism, spelled with a small m, refers to what can be called traces of mannerism in varying historical eras and varying places and can be interpreted as either naïve or sophisticated in its manifestation.

Explicit Mannerism is exemplified in the sixteenth-century work of Giulio Romano, acknowledged as *the* Mannerist architect by historians. But it also embraces the architectural work of Michelangelo and Palladio. Implicit mannerism I also find to be an enduring and endearing characteristic of much English architecture, from Late Gothic to Sir Edwin Lutyens—or was he explicit? This is why I adore and learn from English architecture, from Gloucester Cathedral to Lutyens' manor houses.

122. Gloucester Cathedral, Gloucester, England.

123. Hardwick Hall, Chesterfield, England.

124. Inigo Jones' St. Paul's Church, Covent Garden, London.

IMPLICIT MANNERISM: EXAMPLES

What I am describing as a mannerism to evolve via complexity and contradiction for our time is more on the explicit side than the implicit side—it is more capital M-oriented than small m. But I shall first review some historical examples of implicit mannerist precedent in England that I have subjectively chosen—many of which were illustrated as examples of complexity and contradiction in *Complexity and Contradiction:*

- Gloucester Cathedral, whose buttresses expressed within the walls of the nave are essentially structural and horrendously incorrect, within the hyper-rational architectural order that is Gothic.
- The architecture of most Elizabethan and Jacobean manor houses, whose tense compositions embrace bearing walls that consist mostly of window openings, as well as compositional dualities, iconographic

125, 126.
Sir Christopher
Wren's St. Paul's
Cathedral, London.

127. Sir Christopher Wren's St. Stephen's Walbrook,
London.

signage at the scale of billboards, and stylistic ambiguities. Are they
naïve or sophisticated? Is this Late Gothic or Early Renaissance, as at
Longleat House, Montacute House, Hardwick Hall, Hatfield House?

- Inigo Jones' St. Paul's, Covent Garden, an adorable church as a
  temple, whose incorrect Classical proportions create sublime tension.
- Saint (rather than Sir) Christopher Wren: *viva* St. Paul's Cathedral,
  whose ultimate Baroque dome and drum are supported by a kind of
  incorrect/ambiguous pendentives inside (naïve *and* sophisticated?)!
  And Saint Stephen's Walbrook, whose similar configurations combine convention and originality to create tension!

128. Nicholas Hawksmoor's Christ Church, Spitalfields, London.

129. Nicholas Hawksmoor's St. George's, Bloomsbury, London.

130. Sir John Vanbrugh's Blenheim Palace, Woodstock, England

131. Sir John Soane's House and Museum, London.

- The façade of Nicholas Hawksmoor's Christ Church, Spitalfields: is it a façade or is it a tower? Or his St. George's, Bloomsbury—a symmetrical classical temple but with its huge tower halfway down one side.
- Sir John Vanbrugh's Blenheim Palace, a building I visited on my first day in Europe. On its front façade: is that a broken pediment or a dilatory pediment?
- Sir John Soane's arches inside his house and museum, which are hanging rather than supported.

Similar analyses can be made concerning the work—not original in their vocabularies but valid for their mannerist quality—of other British masters like that of William Butterfield, Charles Rennie Mackintosh, and Lutyens. And could it be argued that some of these Brits were explicit Mannerists?

Other examples—not British—that evoke implicit mannerism with a small m:

- The longitudinal elevations of the interior of Francesco Borromini's Baroque chapel of I Re Magi of the Palazzo di Propaganda Fide, whose piers compose dualities that are then mollified by the corners of the hall as they spatially evolve.
- Luigi Moretti's Casa del Girasole in the Parioli section of Rome, via the duality of its front elevation: is it one building or two? Probably one, because of the inflection atop each of its two segments.
- The plans of Guarino Guarini's Church of the Immaculate Conception in Turin and Giuseppe Vaccaro's San Gregorio Barbarigo in Rome, where each composes at once dualities and wholes.
- Alvar Aalto's church in, Vuoksenniska, near Imatra, involving a conventional but asymmetrical nave as well as contradictory layers inside.

132, 133. Francesco Borromini's I Re Magi chapel, Rome.

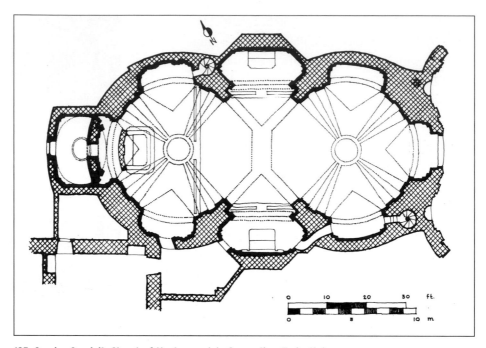

135. Guarino Guarini's Church of the Immaculate Conception, Turin, Italy.

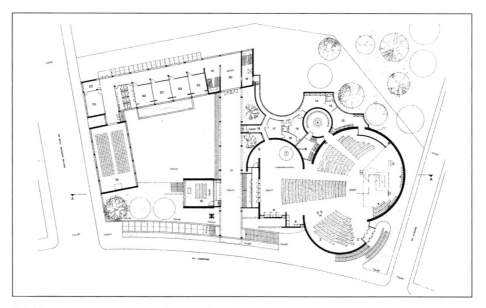

136. Giuseppe Vaccaro's San Gregorio Barbarigo, Rome.

134. Luigi Moretti's Casa del Girasole, Rome.

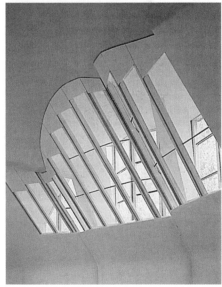

137, 138. Alvar Aalto's church in Vuoksenniska, Imatra, Finland.

140. Cathedral, Cefalù, Sicily.

139. Church of the Jacobins, Toulouse, France.

141. McKim, Mead & White's Low House, Bristol, Rhode Island.

- The Gothic church of the Jacobins in Toulouse, whose row of columns/piers marching mysteriously up the center of the nave make it an example par excellence of duality—and of ambiguous beauty.
- The mosaic figure of Christ in the apse of the cathedral in Cefalù—it is eloquently too big.
- The slopes of the pedimented roof of the Low House, an early work of McKim, Mead & White in Bristol, Rhode Island, which occur on the long elevations and therefore on the "wrong" sides of the house, but the house as iconic shelter is thereby eloquently enhanced.
- And the work of Frank Furness, teeming with ambiguous dualities, as in the Pennsylvania Academy of the Fine Arts and the National Bank for the Republic in Philadelphia. Much of his other work was demolished—for being mannerist?
- And Armando Brasini's Church of the Cuore Immacolato di Maria Santissima in Rome, full of "too muches" and "too littles" in its dynamic classical composition inside and out—not to mention that its name is too long.
- And finally the ultimate example of mannerist *urbanism*—the city of Tokyo itself, whose aesthetic of chaos derives from its revolutionary demolitions and its evolutionary multiculturalism, making it an exemplary city of today!

142. Frank Furness's Pennsylvania Academy of Fine Arts, Philadelphia.

143. Frank Furness's National Bank of the Republic, Philadelphia.

144. Armando Brasini's Church of the Cuore Immacolato di Maria Santissima, Rome.

EXPLICIT MANNERISM: EXAMPLES

Here are some historical examples of explicit Mannerist precedent that I consider relevant and that "turn me on"—many of which also were illustrated as examples of complexity and contradiction in *Complexity and Contradiction*.

First of all, the architectural work of Michelangelo, whom I love the most and learn the most from, and whose architectural work in the sixteenth century, along with Palladio's, I consider explicitly Mannerist. I can refer to the rear façade of St. Peter's, with its grand scale confirmed and yet humanized by the height of its false attic windows, which matches that of the capitals of the adjacent pilasters; to the Laurentian Library, whose interior pilasters are columns individually niched within

 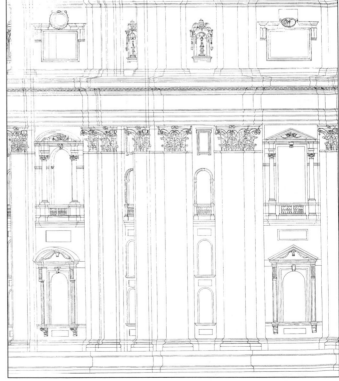

145, 146. Michelangelo's St. Peter's, Rome.

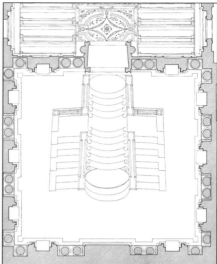

147, 148. Michelangelo's Laurentian Library, Florence.

the wall and whose vestibule is a room and a staircase at the same time; to the façades of the facing buildings of the Capitoline Hill, which, through their giant and minor orders, glorify vagaries of scale and create humane monumentality; to the Sforza Chapel in Santa Maria Maggiore, each of whose side walls as a niche, via its huge radius in plan, makes the space by implication expand beyond itself, and the space is therefore perceived as bigger than it is and therefore as a monumental as well as a small space; to the Porta Pia, with its varying combinations of scales and

149. Michelangelo's Capitoline Hill, Rome.

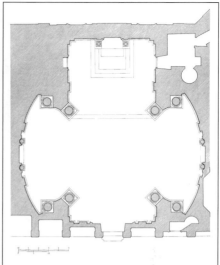

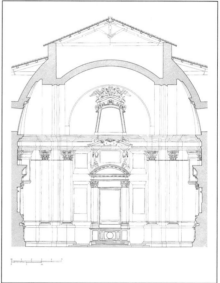

150, 151, 152. Michelangelo's Sforza Chapel, Rome.

153, 154. Michelangelo's Porta Pia, Rome.

symbols and distorted conventions of vocabulary, illustrated on the cover of my controversial book of thirty-eight years ago.

And then there is Palladio, known throughout history more for his architectural good manners via his writings and his villas than for his Mannerism via his palaces and churches. But to me he is a Mannerist in a Mannerist period. How else can you acknowledge the corner of the front façade of the glorious Palazzo Valmarana in Vicenza, whose bay is defined not by the macho pilaster of the giant order that consistently defines the typical rhythmic bay of the rest of the façade but by several small-scale elements—a minor-order pilaster at the ground floor level and a statue in relief as a kind of caryatid at the *piano nobile* level. Also, all but one of the five openings vertically composed in this bay are smaller in size than the three openings of the typical bays that conform to the three stories of the rest of the façade. Corners are usually less rather than more delicate in wall-bearing façades—and the effect of reversing this convention is haunting.

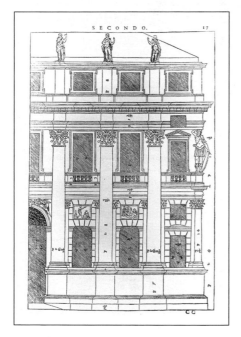

155. Andrea Palladio's Palazzo Valmarana, Vicenza. **156. Andrea Palladio's San Giorgio Maggiore, Venice.** **157. Andrea Palladio's Il Redentore, Venice.**

And then there are the front façades of two of Palladio's churches in Venice—San Giorgio Maggiore and Il Redentore—teeming with complexities and contradictions that are valid. In each case here is a Christian church whose interior is based on a Roman basilica (a law court) and whose exterior is based on a Roman temple—or is it a juxtaposition of temples? And the combination of basilica and temple(s) makes for beautifully weird juxtapositions and layerings on the front, where each side of the basilican façade becomes a bisected fragment of a pedimented temple and where the buttresses of the interior vault become other kinds of fragments of temple pediments. And then the temple's front columns become pilasters of various scales on a wall, and the entrance becomes another little temple façade juxtaposed upon the center. And then the way that some of these elements, involving forms, symbols, and scales, hit the ground, combining bases, no bases, and steps, makes for other elements of architectural wonder in a Mannerist period—the Italian sixteenth century!

158. Traditional Japanese interior.

159. Japanese Buddhist Temple.

MANNERIST ARCHITECTURE AS COMMUNICATION FOR TODAY'S AND TOMORROW'S MULTICULTURALISM: ELECTRONIC ICONOGRAPHY FOR AN ARCHITECTURE AS COMMUNICATION: LEARNING FROM TOKYO

A mannerist architecture of communication can involve learning from Japan—whose historical architecture embraces not only Shinto minimalism, exemplified in the temples and gardens in Kyoto and worshipped and promoted by Modernist theorists of the last century, but also Buddhist complexity, exemplified in the temples of Nikko and ignored by Modernist theorists. Within Japanese architectural culture there is not only a minimalist aesthetic but also a complex and contradictory aesthetic—not only an apparently abstract aesthetic but also an explicitly symbolic aesthetic.

A mannerist architecture of communication also involves learning from Tokyo—a city of *now*, a city of valid chaos rather than minimalist order. So we go from Rome, to Las Vegas, to Tokyo—to a city largely rebuilt in the last half-century, combining both revolutionary grandeur and evolutionary pragmatism. It juxtaposes within pre-war

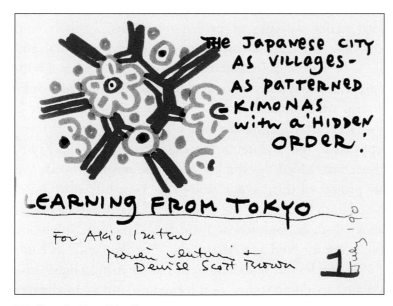

160. "Learning From Tokyo."

161. Japanese street.

162. Building in Tokyo.

163. Tokyo street.

street patterns and property lines both rural shrines and global headquarters, sidewalk markets and Corbusian high-rises, all exuding vitality. Combining urban mannerist qualities with an architecture as commercial communication, Tokyo is even more horrible—I mean wonderful—than America's commercial manifestations of it: I refer to all those Japanese pencil buildings whose façades become frameworks for signs, and thereby consist solely of patterns of balconies as signs. And then there's the Baroque-like Ginza—a Times Square radiating and celebrating architecture as communication for day and night.

A mannerist architecture of communication can involve learning from New York City—from two recently erected buildings that exemplify architecture as communication for today, buildings we would love to have been the architects of: the Morgan Stanley Building on Broadway between 49th and 50th Streets, and the Morgan Stanley Dean Witter Building on Seventh Avenue and 50th Street. The lower portion of the former building emits from its façade changing verbal information via its pixilated medium and is thereby vitally ornamental *and* explicitly useful within its setting. The latter building—via its LED medium—radiates, indeed exalts, varieties of evolving patterns, symbols, and words that combine changing elements of content, ornamental and informational. As backgrounds for electronic media, the façades of both buildings are architecturally conventional. The latter is eloquently ordinary with its strip windows and absence of formal articulations: it is appropriately a Decorated Shed rather than a Duck.

We are happy that the architects for the latter building, Kohn, Pederson & Fox, have added this dimension to the neighborhood. We remember our project of thirty-some years ago for a fifty-story hotel between 45th and 46th Streets, for the west side of Broadway, in association with Emory Roth & Sons, whose front façade included integrally a sixty-foot-high sign for bold advertisements. *Viva* the façade as computer screen! *Viva* façades not reflecting light but emanating light—the building as a digital sparkling source of information, not as an abstract glowing source of light!

164. Kohn Pederson Fox's Morgan Stanley Building, New York.

168. VSBA's hotel project, New York.

165, 166, 167. Kohn Pederson Fox's Morgan Stanley Dean Witter Building, New York.

169. Times Square, New York.

Here, we are learning from the Piazza San Marco *and* from Times Square. The proximity of these two buildings to Times Square is significant because is not Times Square *the* significant urban space of our time—the equivalent of the Piazza San Marco of an earlier time? Here, the richness of combined scales, pedestrian and vehicular, and of commercial architecture as communication deriving from electrical and electronic signage corresponds to the richness at a pedestrian scale of

170. Piazza San Marco, Venice.

combined styles of commercial, civic, and religious architecture of the piazza. And is not the sense of community deriving from spatial and symbolic qualities of the piazza an equivalent to the sense of community deriving from the changing/dynamic messages that electronic technology affords? Right after September 11th, varieties of relevant messages enhanced Times Square as a dynamic communal place. And so we go from static tesserae to changing pixels for a complex multicultural age that engages both vulgar communication and vital mannerism!

And then there is learning from Federation Square in Melbourne, as described by William Mitchell: "[The] focal point isn't a monument or a

171. Times Square, New York.

172. San Vitale, Ravenna, Italy.

stage. It's a giant LED screen showing, when I was there, tennis live from the Australian Open . . . It works: the crowds are there in the numerous open-air cafes, contentedly sipping cappuccinos. It goes beyond straight-forward appropriation from Mother Earth and Mother Country to con-front—boldly and mostly successfully—the problem of public space for a postcolonial, multicultural, electronically networked society."[5]

So, *viva* electronic pixels over decorative rivets! *Viva* iconography—not carved in stone for eternity but digitally changing for *now*, so that the inherently dangerous fascist propaganda, for instance, can be tem-porarily, not eternally, proclaimed!

And let us acknowledge that electronics for architectural surfaces is an expensive medium but also that the price of this technology is dimin-ishing by the month. And let us recognize and respect as well the cul-tural obligations for no iconography—in the case of synagogues and Quaker meeting houses, for example.

A last example of explicit architectural Mannerism for the twenty-first century—that of the Sainsbury Wing of the National Gallery in London. Here is an example of explicit Mannerism much misunder-stood in its time. The historical revivalists say the building design is not correct, and the Modernists say it's not Modern. It is a building whose non-ideological/pragmatic complexity and contradiction derive from its context as an addition to William Wilkins's National Gallery of the 1830s and as an element reinforcing the spatial and symbolic signifi-cance of Trafalgar Square. Each of the four façades is different—to accommodate the context of the street or square it faces—involving the Miesian glass curtain wall to the east, the severe brick-faced "back" walls to the north and west, and the limestone façade to the south, accommo-dating to the Square on the right and Pall Mall South on the left.

It is significant that the principal façade, which is Mannerist-Classical in white limestone, is perceived in itself as a sign (a billboard?) facing the Square, since right around the corner of the building one cannot avoid seeing the contrasting Miesian glass curtain wall with its black frame-work. And the principal façade, as a continuation of Wilkins's original façade, is both like the original and not like it. The surface material is the same, and the Classical vocabulary of the architectural elements is the same, deriving from precise replications of the original elements and positioned vertically in the same ways. But the horizontal positioning of the elements is significantly different, so that rhythmic relationships are contrasting, especially in the positioning of the pilasters. The rhythm of the compositional elements of the original building can be said to be that of a gavotte or a minuet while that of the new wing is contemporary jazzy; the former is lyrical in its expression, the latter dissonant. And the asymmetrical composition of these elements works to create compositional inflection—an inflection of the new façade toward the old façade so that the new building is in itself a fragment within a whole and would make no architectural sense if it were standing alone.

Another contrast between the old and the new is the bigger entrance of the latter, which works as an intrusion within the order of the composition to accommodate the millions of visitors annually anticipated for the new wing instead of the thousands for which the old wing was designed, while the decorative colonnettes work to mollify the scale of the new entrance. And then there is the big window along Pall Mall West whose scale expresses the civic quality of this building. It is these complexities and contradictions that work to promote harmony between the old and the new and the varying contexts—via analogy and contrast within a difficult whole.

Viva modest mannerism over pseudo-Modernism—or flashy Modernism or abstract expressionism or Baroque vulgarity. *Viva* convention and ambiguity over strange originality for a mannerism of now! *Viva* ambiguity acknowledged unambiguously!

Vincent Scully wrote in 1989: "There can be little doubt that the art of illusion, the art of the television screen and of electronic fantasy, will play a considerable role in the architecture of the future, much as painting and sculpture did in the architecture of the past."[6] Perhaps the appropriate use of computers for architecture in an Electronic Age is not to compose contorted forms but to validate valid surfaces, for an Information Age.

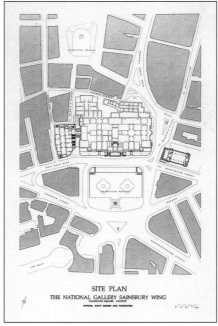

173, 174, 175, 176. Sainsbury Wing, National Gallery, London.

Architecture as Patterns and Systems

Learning from Planning

DENISE SCOTT BROWN

— 5 —
Some Ideas and Their History

Bob and I stress communication and iconography when we write and lecture, but in designing and building we spend ninety percent of our time on other issues. These other issues are the subject of this part of the book. In describing some lesser-known aspects of our work, I hope to counter the stereotypes about us, to demonstrate that there's much beyond neon in our philosophy, and to reiterate that we are not Postmodernists and never were.[1] The origins of our thinking are more complex than that.

Although I can't cover everything we think of in our practice, my aim in these essays is to point to some ideas that I feel are basic to our work. Derived, many of them, from urban planning, they have allowed our firm to practice in areas beyond architecture, but they have also helped us to do our main job, architecture, in a somewhat different way.

In conveying complex thoughts that we've absorbed, evolved, and used over a lifetime, it may help to describe their origins historically or even personally, to clarify them and show their place in a scheme of things. For this reason, I'll make the professional personal for a moment, showing the origins of my thinking in my early experiences in Africa and Europe and my education in urban planning in America.

Mine is an African view of Las Vegas

Our thinking has many sources. Mine started in Africa—perhaps before. The 1910–1929 volume of *Oeuvres Complètes* opens with a letter Le Corbusier wrote in 1936 to Rex Martienssen, leader of a group of young architects, aspirant Modernists, working in Johannesburg, South Africa. My mother was at architecture school with them. After her second year she could not afford to continue but, when she married, she hired her friends to design our house. This was in 1934. I think ours was the

177. This Modern house is where I grew up. I climbed its steel columns and played ships on its spiral stair and deck. You can have mythic allusions in houses with flat roofs, and you can also play on the roof.

178. This shows the African rural life that paralleled ours. The contrast between the two was ever present in South Africa.

second International Style house in Johannesburg, but we would not have called it that; to us it was Modern. We moved in when I was four years old. Before I was four, I saw its plans. I remember blueprints—really *blue* prints. The house was designed by Hansen, Tomkin, and Finkelstein. Their work is illustrated in journals of the time. It was a truly beautiful house.

So I have personal and familial attachments to early Modernism, and I claim our architecture continues in that vein—updated, of course, for today. When, in the 1960s, we reacted against Modern architecture, it was not the early tradition that we described as decadent but its development in the 1950s and 1960s, which we felt lacked the clarity and verve of its 1920s and 1930s forebears.

A second African route to my themes in architecture took me via Las Vegas. Mine is an African view of Las Vegas. To explain, I must return to Johannesburg in the 1940s. This was a multicultural society, a work center for Africans from across the continent but also a refuge from Nazism for Europeans, many of them Jews. It was a sophisticated center of the arts. Growing up there, I had an art teacher, Rosa van Gelderen, a Dutch Jewish refugee, who said, "You will not be a creative artist if you don't paint what's around you." She meant the life of Africans in the streets of Johannesburg. She made me notice where I was and awoke my interest in popular culture. I was about ten.

No child in South Africa could be unaware of the agonized issues of justice and equity between the races there. But artistically our location had another side. Our distance from the centers of European culture made us feel out of touch, especially during World War II; yet being at a periphery raised challenging questions: Where did we fit, culturally and artistically? With Africa or with England?

For example, we made Christmas cards in school—there's multiculturalism for you: a Jewish child painting Christmas cards. In this English-based school, we painted snow scenes in Surrey. This was in the middle of the South African summer. An extreme version of such colonial cultural domination was a film showing young black French West Africans reciting lessons on "nos ancêtres les Gaulois"—our ancestors the Gauls (I learned in France, later, that they no longer do that). These early African experiences first raised the polarity of "is" and "ought" for me. Here it was the "is" of the "colony" and the "ought" of the "mother country," and it could be translated artistically into a question: What environment lies around us, and how is this different from what the media of the dominant culture (mostly English) suggest should be there?

The South African author Dan Jacobson wrote that he had never seen his own karoo landscape in a book until he read *The Story of an*

179. This was the kind of African urban scene my art teacher thought we should paint.

180. But this other landscape is what we discovered ourselves. When we returned from England, Robert Scott Brown and I began taking photographs of African popular culture. This shows African blankets for sale in a rural store in Natal. Note the multicultural signs—Zulu, English, and American.

181. This beautiful African urbanism is a village of the Mapoch tribe. On the gateposts are Mapoch interpretations of Western suburban houses. Beside them are Gillette razor blade patterns.

182. This is an African interpretation of the city of Bulawayo in Zimbabwe: high-rise buildings and a train station.

African Farm by Olive Schreiner. He suggested that the surprise discovery of your familiar surroundings in print is part of the African experience.[2] As a child, I too saw almost exclusively English places in the books I read. I lived in a harsher, drier landscape and, although I found the high veld incredibly beautiful, English people around me seemed to like it only to the extent that it reminded them of "home." Why, I wondered, must my landscape look like Surrey to be beautiful? And I became an African xenophobe.

But my xenophobia was only half right. There is a necessity, I now believe, to relate immediate circumstances to a broader tradition, perhaps to several. Nevertheless, learning-from-what's-around-you has remained an overarching theme for me, and seeing how African artists confronted that theme was important to me, growing up.

The clash of cultures in South Africa, although politically dreadful, was artistically exciting and invigorating. African folk artists' interpretations of Western artifacts had unbounded vitality.[3] They were much more interesting than the Western artists' responses to African cultures. African folk art that incorporated Western images was decried by the purists but I found it fascinating. It prepared me for the impurity of Las Vegas.

Think before you judge

In 1952 I left South Africa to spend my fourth year—our architecture school's practicum year—in an architect's office in London. I never went back.

Instead, I entered the Final School at the Architectural Association (the AA) in London. I landed in post–World War II England amidst the look-back-in-anger generation, in a society in upheaval, where social activism was part of education. A friend at the AA had a major scholarship from his hometown, while his brother had left school just before the war, at fourteen. Social change of that magnitude affected everything, including art. On the one hand, there was the frou-frou of the Festival of Britain, and on the other, socialism.[4]

Out of the clash came innovative social thought and ideas on rebuilding London. The sociologists Michael Young and Peter Willmott studied the people of London's East End and described what happened when they were moved to new towns outside the city. Before Jane Jacobs, Young and Willmott voiced complaints against the social disruption induced by urban planning.[5]

Loosely allied to the social thinkers was an assemblage of avant-garde London artists called the Independent Group. Within that group were members of a proto Pop Art movement, dating from the early *1940s*— and also the architects Alison and Peter Smithson, founders of New Brutalism, a movement of the 1950s and 1960s that related architecture to social realism.

The Smithsons came from the north of England, another periphery. They became involved in the London East End, yet another periphery. In England in the 1950s, an equivalent to the African colonial vs. mother country debate was a working-class vs. upper-middle-class debate. This, too, involved "is" and "ought," but here the reality to learn from was the street life of the East End. The Smithsons talked about "active socio-plastics," but only briefly; later they said you couldn't get much help from sociologists and took another tack. I stayed with socio-plastics.

In my second year at the AA, I joined a group of students whose views paralleled those of the Smithsons. They shared my interest in early Modern architecture—as Peter Smithson said, we "caught a whiff of the powder" of that earlier revolution. These students loved the American grain elevators that Le Corbusier loved and English nineteenth-century brick factory buildings, but they were turning, as well, toward commercial architecture, seeing there further opportunities for iconoclastic vitality. We started taking snapshots. Long before visiting Las Vegas, I was photographing popular culture and everyday landscapes and their signage in Africa, Europe, and England.

The New Brutalists joined with Team 10, an international group that shared their ideals, in energetically upending the prevailing 1950s architectural ideology, which they felt had veered from true Modernism.[6] They saw themselves as loyal Modernists, upholding the tradition but updating it to meet postwar realities. First, they returned to the early Modern "functionalist" revolution, the one I had identified with. The German Moderns' term, *Neue Sachlichkeit*, new objectivity, describes what they were after and what I have continued to strive for. In effect, they said, "If you look very straight at a problem, the solution you find may be ugly, but that ugliness may be right."

The architect Louis I. Kahn later said much the same thing: "You hate it and you hate it and you hate it, until you love it, because it's the way it has to be." There's a moral case for this argument, but there's an aesthetic one too. Looking objectively at problems, considering the merits of ugly but effective solutions, can help artists open their eyes, escape from aesthetic ruts, and enhance their creativity. This approach suggests, "Don't judge at first," but it was understood by some to mean, "Don't judge at all." For me it means, "Think before you judge."

I was influenced, as well, by Arthur Korn, my studio critic and advisor at the AA. Through his teaching and his book *History Builds the Town*, he tried to show how the social life and history of an era affected its building.

But my English friends were going from liking the uncomfortably direct solution to savoring the uncomfortably *in*direct one: to

Mannerism. Mannerist breaking of rules seemed relevant not as an expression of neurosis (an earlier interpretation) but as a way of approaching the complexity of life. Combining Mannerism and *Neue Sachlichkeit* suggested that breaking aesthetic rules to meet functional exigencies could produce aesthetic excitement.

In 1956 and 1957 Robert Scott Brown, my first husband, and I traveled in Europe. We planned our itinerary around Mannerist and early Modern architecture, and headed toward Venice to attend a CIAM Summer School, held there for young architects from around the world.[7] CIAM in 1956 was in a stage of dissolution following the revolt of the young Turks of Team 10. Nevertheless, the summer school brought together an array of vital people who represented all CIAM trends. There were elderly, old-line Modernists, mainstream Modernists in mid-career, and young members mostly allied with Team 10. Robert and I were moved to hear from some architects, Franco Albini for one, what a beacon of hope Modernism had been for them during Fascist times.

The themes of the summer school were the same postwar issues faced by the Brutalists, but the lecturers' and organizers' responses to them had an Italian accent. For all groups, the continuity of the Modern Movement—*continuità*—was a major consideration. They, as we, saw their job as loyally pushing Modern architecture to become relevant to postwar conditions. However, in Italy there was much more discussion of tradition and heritage than there had been among the Brutalists, and their take on *Neue Sachlichkeit* and the realities of urban life had to do with pre-industrial and peasant societies rather than with an urban mass society and the scale of industry.

We preferred the tougher-minded Brutalist approach and found ourselves at bay in arguments with middle-aged Italian architects, amused by us and in sympathy with our passion but puzzled over its focus on the jarring signs and scales of commercial and industrial architecture. They smiled ironically at what they considered our hoary technological romanticism, but I think they were remembering their youth.

The architect Ludovico Quaroni helped us find temporary work in Rome in the winter of 1956, in the studio of Giuseppe Vaccaro, who was described as "a very serious architect." Vaccaro had need of two draftspeople for six weeks to help meet the deadline for a project for INA-Casa in the Tiburtino quarter of Rome. Here began a lifelong association with Italy and with the Vaccaros. We found Vaccaro's tough but warmhearted rationalism and his dour, small houses, carefully tied to the lives of their users, "almost"—we were young and arrogant!—up to our high, Brutalist standards.

In his design, Vaccaro played with the meshing of several systems. Each was derived within its own logic but, in combination, they made a greater whole. There was no bombast, nothing was overdone, yet the design purveyed the sense of a society progressing and urbanizing. I think we learned more from Vaccaro than we could have from other architects, whose more famous Tiburtino designs lacked this rationalist edge and seemed simply allusive to traditional societies. Working for Vaccaro helped prepare us for urbanism in America.[8]

We returned to South Africa in 1957 and spent some months traveling and working there. Our photographs from that time are of Cape Dutch, Natal English, and urban vernacular architecture; African housing, rural and urban; and folk and popular culture. By 1958, when we left for America, our voyage of study and discovery had transmuted into something else. I felt I had found my feet in architecture and developed my major themes. These themes—still my concerns and the subject of this book—were to be greatly influenced by my next few years of study at the University of Pennsylvania.

We couldn't believe we had lived our lives till then without what we had just learned

Peter Smithson said the only place to study in America was at the University of Pennsylvania, because Louis Kahn taught there. So Robert Scott Brown and I went to Penn to study with Kahn. We arrived with our Brutalist rhetoric, and Kahn seemed to know all about it. He had met the Brutalists and Team 10 and, for a while, there was a confluence of ideas among them. Kahn's Richards Medical Laboratory seems to me to be based on the Open Air School in Amsterdam by Johannes Duiker. This was an icon of the Brutalists.[9]

We chose to enter Penn's Department of City Planning because, in 1950s England and Europe, planning was considered the basis for architecture. If you were a committed and talented young architect, the next step was to study city planning, but the training in England was too prosaic. On reaching Penn we found, to our surprise, that Kahn did not teach in the planning department. Our student advisor, the architect and planner David Crane, said, "Don't worry, I'll make sure you get the best of Kahn but, coming from Africa and talking as you do, you should have city planning training. You need that for where you're going." We were going back to work in Africa as Africans.[10]

After the first semester in planning, we couldn't believe we had lived our lives till then without what we had just learned. One example was Herbert Gans's urban sociology course. When we met him, Gans had just moved to Levittown, New Jersey, to be a participant-observer in the birth of the community. The London East End study was on his course reading list, and he had recently completed a parallel study of the Boston West End, recording the experiences of its inhabitants under urban renewal.

Gans's critique of urban renewal predates that of Jane Jacobs and is broader and more scholarly. When I assess scholarship in our field, my yardstick is Gans. He culled the themes of his course from several disciplines. Perhaps from psychiatry came the notion of being nonjudgmental. Gans recommended that urban planners reserve judgment on urban phenomena—at least at first—to make subsequent judgment more sensitive and to ensure that recommendations derive from an open-minded understanding of the situation. Again, "is" and "ought" came up. How far should the "ought" of the recommendation diverge from the "is" of what exists? Gans had us read the sociologist Robert Merton on functionalism and introduced us to the question, "Functional for whom?"

Another theme was action and reaction. In urban development, the public sector may act then the private sector react, or vice versa. Social thinkers at Penn set this kinetic notion of city building, with its focus on sequence and the roles of many players, against the traditional view of architect-controlled "master planning."

Social scientists' perceptions of urban form were fascinating to me as an architect. Behind their reasoning lay the belief that there are regularities to be understood in society and in the behavior of people. The journey to work, for example, is a regular pattern in urban life. Urban economists, particularly regional scientists, developed hypothetical geometries of urban settlement, based on variables such as travel time, the cost of movement, the location of raw materials, and the premise "Here is nearer than there." They laid gossamer patterns over the land to depict relationships between these variables. I found these patterns beautiful and evocative—as evocative as the plans of indigenous villages in Africa and Europe that the Brutalists and Team 10 loved to study. I learned to pore over maps and aerial photographs—even over demographic tables, which I had not thought could be interesting—seeking in them signs of order and pointers toward form, aiming as a designer to evolve order from within rather than impose it from above.

The social planners are still my conscience and many of their methods are my methods

In the early 1960s, social and physical scientists were concerned with complex systems, and urban economists and transportation planners were initiating the use of computers in regional planning. The inappropriate simplifications they made in applying computers to cities caused me to try to keep up with them, to make sure they didn't do silly things. So while I was teaching at Penn I audited further courses in sociology, regional science, economic development, decision theory, planning theory, computer theory, traffic planning, and urban transportation modeling.

With the Civil Rights movement, some urban social scientists became social activists, and the field of social planning was defined. At Penn this change started in the late 1950s.[11] In the 1960s, evolving ideas on the connection between politics and planning—particularly theories on democratic participation of the poor in planning—added new dimensions to the planners' views of urban development as an oscillation, an action and reaction, between the public and the private sectors. "Is" and "ought" figured in the social planners' critique of urban renewal, as they raised the question, "Who benefits and who loses through the decisions of planners?"

In the early 1960s the social planners launched a mighty attack on architects. In this, they were not simon-pure. Granted, the architects were often wrong, but the planners were imperialists. They forged into urban planning partly because there was money from Washington to confront urban social problems via urban renewal. When they found architects in possession of the turf, the planners pushed hard on them, deriding their philosophies of urbanism.

Yet architects' plans for the city *were* part of the problem. Given their unsophisticated ideas on what constituted doing good and their physical bias—their belief that every problem must have a physical solution—architects as urbanists were far from achieving the social goals their rhetoric proclaimed. Even in the 1990s, when Architects, Designers, and Planners for Social Responsibility, a deeply caring organization, considered how best to act on their social concern, they decided to design a "Peace Park."

I was much in sympathy with the social planning movement and agreed with its activism and its evolving theory; yet I fought the social planners over their simplification of architecture and planning. "I've actually done some planning," I said, "It doesn't work quite the way you say it does." Meanwhile, there was furor all around. Riots in cities were the backdrop to the passionate debate on social vs. physical planning that took place in Penn's planning department in the early 1960s.

In it all, Bob Venturi seemed to be the only architect on the Penn faculty who understood. Most said, "How can you go with those churlish social planners?" Even Kahn said, "Sociologists believe in 2.5 people, how can you believe in them?" But the social planners are still my conscience, and many of their methods are my methods.

Urban design was a lowly art
At Penn, and in most places where it was taught and practiced, urban design wore the aesthetic and theoretical hand-me-downs of architecture. David Crane was a major protagonist in the struggle to get urban design beyond architecture's discarded clothing. He was also one of the few members of the Penn faculty who tried to maintain the link between architecture and social-sciences-based, "non-physical" (as they called it) urban planning. It was he who set me to study regional science. He had lived in Nigeria and was interested, as I was, in planning for developing areas. Some of his ideas on Third World urbanism could, I believe, be applied to American cities. Crane defined "Four Faces of Movement," describing the street as a city builder, a giver of access, a room (particularly if you think of Indian or Italian cities), and a communicator of information in the city. In the late 1950s he wrote on the city's ability to communicate through the symbolism of its form, and in 1961 he persuaded me to write an article, "The Meaningful City."[12] For me, it was another point of departure for Las Vegas.

Crane was interested in change within the city. How can you plan for it when you can't predict it? He criticized planners who say, "Here is the low projection, here is the high projection; we'll build in the middle." Crane asked us to think of ways of planning that would enable cities and buildings to adapt to unpredictable change. This involved a reassessment of the architectural philosophy of functionalism.

Although Louis Kahn didn't trust the sociologists, much of his urbanism reverberated, I feel, to Penn's planning school. If you go behind Kahn's beautiful diagrams for Philadelphia's movement systems, you see the ideas of Robert B. Mitchell, a noted planner and transportation strategist at Penn. Kahn's notion of "wanting to be"—as in "The concert hall wants to be a Stradivarius"—would have horrified the sociologists; nevertheless, it entailed looking deep into a problem and evolving a design system from within, rather than imposing one from above. This was true of his work at Bryn Mawr College and in Dacca, Bangladesh, where Kahn developed his thought on buildings as cities in miniature. The complex components of these projects echo the many building themes—the typologies—of a city. He defined the circulation element of a building as "a building within a building" and as a street running through the building. He considered this street to be the common room of the students. Taking the street through the building; allowing for movement, flows and eddies, crossroads, and places for stopping; doing land use and transportation planning *inside* buildings— these became themes of our architecture. They owe to Crane, Kahn, and transportation planning.

When I arrived at Penn in 1958, Kahn was reassessing architectural history under the tutelage of a young architect, Robert Venturi. The influence, despite how history has been written, went mainly from the younger to the older. I took one studio with Kahn and fought him all the way—I think it was a good fight, and it continued during our years as colleagues in Philadelphia.

Robert Venturi and I met as faculty members at Penn in 1960 at my first School of Fine Arts faculty meeting, when I made an impassioned plea that the university not tear down the Furness Library—can you imagine they were considering it? The faculty voted against demolishing it. After the meeting Bob introduced himself, "I agreed with everything you said. My name's Robert Venturi." And I replied, "If you agreed with me, why didn't you say something?"

Our commonality had to do with design, architectural and urban, and how we might respond as designers to concerns we held in common— pluralism, multiculturalism, social activism, symbolism, iconography, impure art, Pop Art, popular culture, the everyday American landscape, Italy, Mannerism, the uses and misuses of history, the uncomfortably direct design solution, and the uncomfortably indirect design solution. We taught parallel courses at Penn. I ran an introductory course on theories of planning, landscape, and architecture, setting up a series of faculty

— 6 —
Activities as Patterns

The activities of people in cities and buildings can be seen as patterns. This chapter discusses patterns urban planners must understand in order to plan, and it surveys some theoretical diagrams evolved by economists and regional scientists to explain the shapes of urban settlements. These have been an evocative muse for us. I show how we have used them, and the ideas behind them, in urban research, urban and campus planning, and the design of buildings.

URBAN PATTERNS, URBAN HYPOTHESES

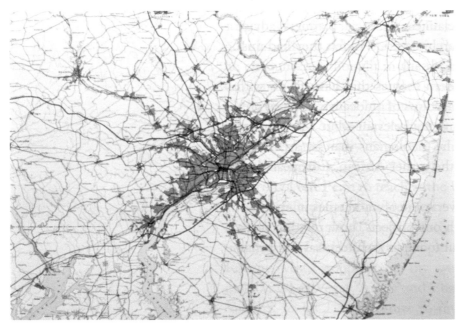

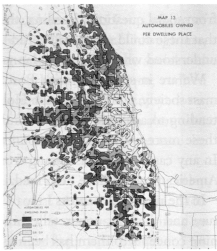

184. This pre-computer map from the Chicago Area Transportation Study, 1959, diagrams transportation-related regularities. The graphics from this study are as beautiful as Klee paintings, and to me represent the same possibilities as Klee's did of combining mathematics and fantasy.

183. Form, Forces, and Function—the City of Philadelphia, 1950. Nineteenth- and early twentieth-century urban form was railroad-dependent.

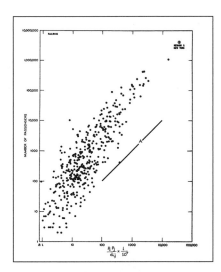

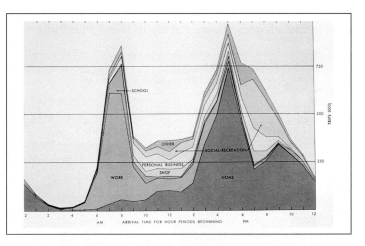

186. An illustration of the "principle of least effort." Some function of size and distance dictates degrees of relationship between 29 different pairs of cities and generates a regular distribution of points on the graph.

185. More regularities: urban travel, primarily the journey to work. The two poles are home and work. A few more people come home at night than go to work in the morning. The dip in the middle is lunchtime.

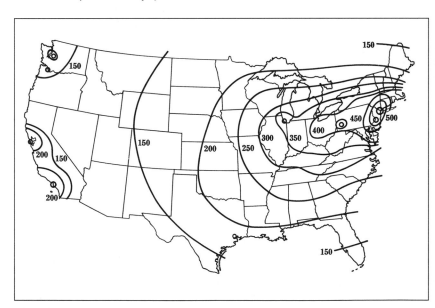

187. The notion of potential: the intensity of influence of New York City.

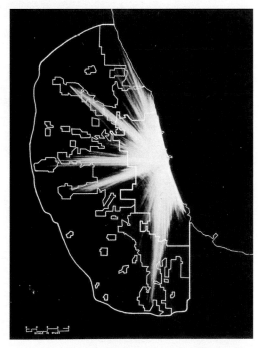

188. The desire lines of people going from home to work.

The notion that form follows forces shows starkly in these illustrations.

189. Kwazulu: an aerial view of a subsistence economy—no roads, no train.

190. Philadelphia: an advanced, trading economy held together by its movement systems.

191. In a city, density is conditioned by geometry. When everyone wants to be at the center, at the market place, they face the problem that, in a circle, there is less area at the center than at the edges. We get hysteria at the center and anemia at the periphery. Theorists of regional science, starting in the early nineteenth century, pondered the effect of the geometry of the circle on agricultural crop-growing patterns.

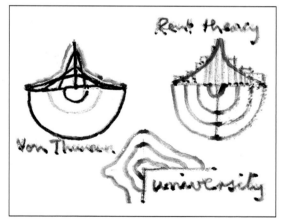

192. Rent theory, which developed from these ideas, posits patterns of density, "rent tents," which look like the New York skyline before the World Trade Center was built, which is when I drew this diagram. This pattern is, I believe, basic. But it distorts. If at the center of town there's a lake, as in Chicago, or a university, as at Princeton, the pattern adjusts around it. But there's always a marketplace, a center of activity, of highest accessibility, even if it becomes multiple centers, as in Los Angeles.

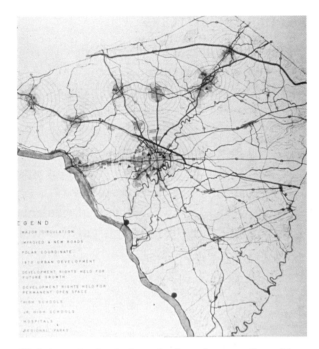

193. In Lancaster County, Pennsylvania, we trace a pattern of towns set concentrically around a regional market center—a "central place."

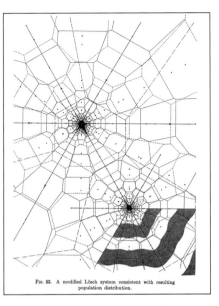

Fig. 52. A modified Lösch system consistent with resulting population distribution.

194. Lösch used hexagons to relate Christaller's conceptual geometry of central places to a landscape. Lancaster County follows the regional scientists' principles to some extent, perhaps even today.

195. The complexity of the land-use pattern of central Philadelphia—and these are only ground floor uses. As Chester Rapkin, my professor of urban economics, used to say, "It looks like a bruise."

196. The complexity of Las Vegas and the Strip; you can see the casinos.

These are two patterns we've pored over considerably. We found them intriguing and sensed their relevance to us as designers, but in order to understand them and eventually contribute to them we had to take them apart first.

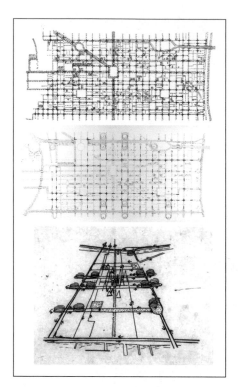

TRANSLATING THE PATTERNS

Here, Kahn and we have taken analytic cross-cuts through the city, isolating one variable for study—Kahn, a movement system, and we, a system of signs. Each exists within a pattern of streets. Disaggregating data in this way—examining the city as a set of patterns formed by a series of interrelated subsystems—can clarify the patterns and may help us to detect new ones. By superimposing a few of the cross-cuts, we move the process from analysis to synthesis. This is an important step toward design—but only if the variables are selected creatively.

The illustrations that follow show analyses and syntheses of elements of the Las Vegas Strip of circa 1968. Very little of this environment remains today.

197. Louis Kahn evolved ideas about movement systems by looking hard at another Philadelphia pattern, one that has been deeply evocative for us too—William Penn's grid plan for the city. By separating different types of movement onto different streets, Kahn converts the grid to a plaid.

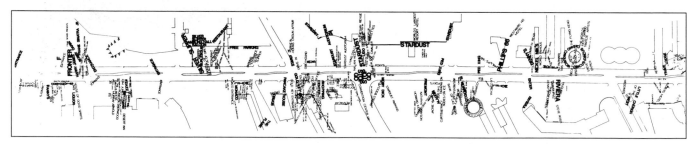

198. We documented every sign on the Strip, trying to understand signage as a system through studying the patterns it created. We saw the Strip as a series of overlaid patterns evolving from the systems—economic, social, natural, and physical—at work on it.

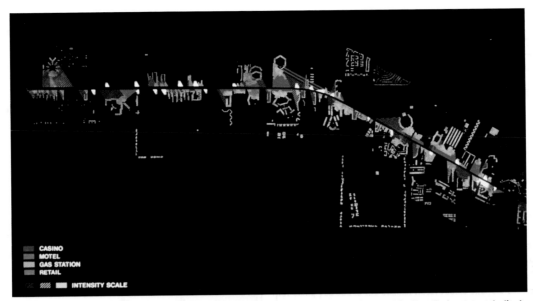

CASINO
MOTEL
GAS STATION
RETAIL
INTENSITY SCALE

200. The Strip as a system of communication: this map suggests how the neon communicates. It also suggests lively intensity.

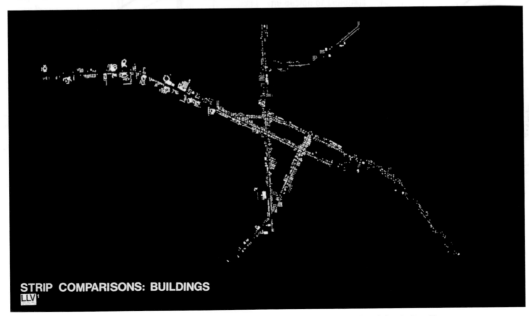

STRIP COMPARISONS: BUILDINGS
LLV'

199. The footprint of every building on the Strip and on several other commercial strips in Las Vegas.

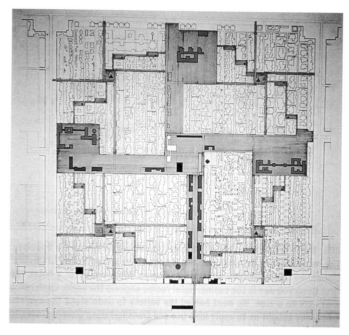

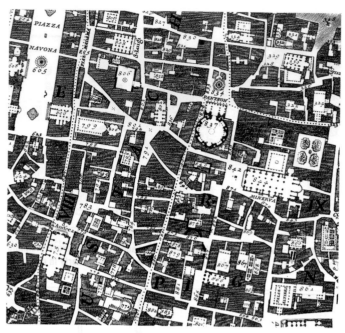

209. David Crane's notion of the capital web. This plan suggests that government may define a grid of facilities and streets and the private sector may react within it.

210. This led us rather directly to Nolli, who mapped the churches of Rome in 1748. The pochéd plans show some unique buildings–churches–of the public sector. You can call them ducks if you like. The white areas are the public open space. The private sector is hatched gray. Nolli made the public structure of Rome apparent.

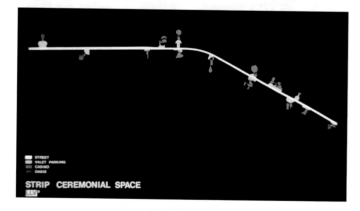

STRIP CEREMONIAL SPACE
LLV'

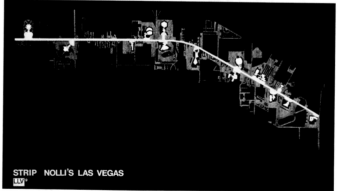

STRIP NOLLI'S LAS VEGAS
LLV'

211, 212. We began making "Nolli" maps of Las Vegas. There is no public sector on the Strip–actually there is a small one–but we show the insides of the casinos, the ceremonial spaces, as a proto-public sector. Again, the public–or, you could say, the semi-public–structure stands out.

USING THE PATTERNS: PUBLIC AND PRIVATE

The early syntheses, the first choices of variables to combine, are the first steps in design. Here are two projects where public and private were important variables to study, and where the relations between them were a major theme in determining the site plan and the building design.

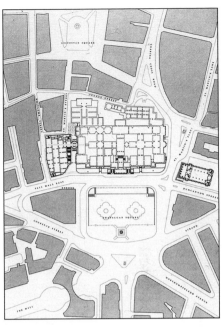

213. Louis Kahn defines a public structure inside his Bryn Mawr dormitory building. He organizes private dormitory rooms to form three communal spaces at the center of the building.

214. Public and private at the Sainsbury Wing. A Nolli map of Trafalgar Square and its environs shows the National Gallery as a large public institution. To the left, VSBA's Sainsbury Wing, opened in 1991, has a grid of spaces that is a smaller version of the one in the main building—smaller, less directive in its arrangements, and more modern.

215. Political demonstration on Trafalgar Square in front of the Sainsbury Wing.

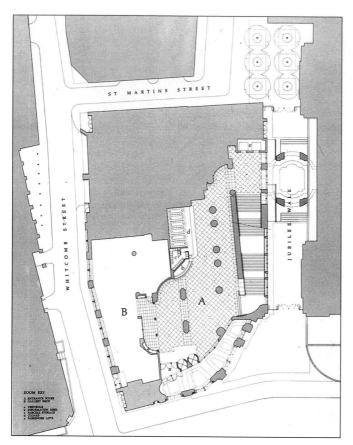

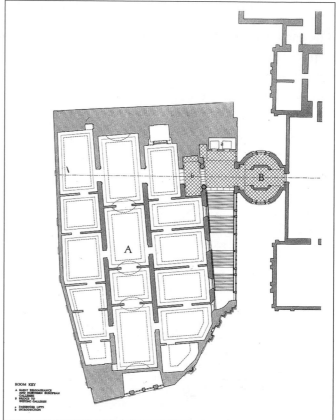

216. A Nolli map of the ground floor of the Sainsbury Wing shows some areas of this public institution to be relatively private. The highly public entry to the building leads to a "street" that progresses through the building. On the ground floor, it is a sinuous worm that can take the flow of a Sunday crowd of thousands of people. The walls of the street are faced in rusticated stone, as an important Renaissance street would be.

217, 218. The "street" travels up the stairway, joins the cross-axis from the main building, and ends with a trompe l'oeil vista across the grid of the galleries.

FROM SYSTEMS TO A DESIGN

The University of Pennsylvania Master Plan and the Perelman Quadrangle,
   1988–2000

We were first planners for the overall campus, then designers of a major increment of the plan. The design for Perelman Quadrangle evolved during our master-planning studies and resulted from an examination of the subsystems of the campus as they related to its historic center.

219. The University of Pennsylvania campus.

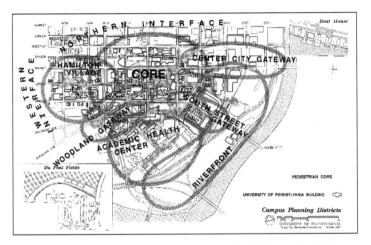

220. This was part of our 1988-1994 master plan study. It helped to define nodes and conjunctions of activity on campus.

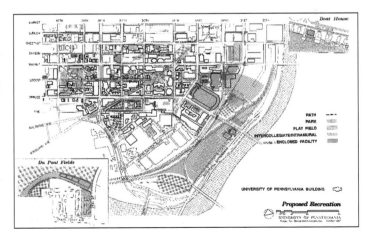

221. Penn's open space system crosses and links its precincts.

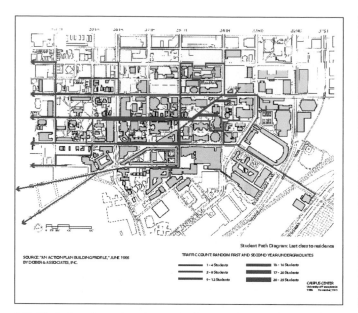

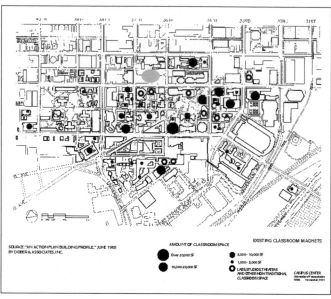

222. Students going and coming: we took a sampling of their rosters and plotted their trips from home to class and vice versa. Their pathways bring you near, but not to, the old center, which was underused.

223. We mapped the distribution of classrooms on campus and noticed that the largest classroom building, Williams Hall, was right beside the old center but not easily accessible to it.

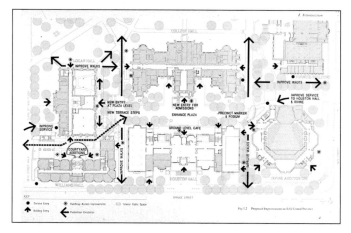

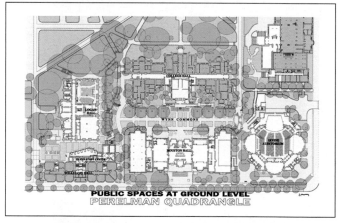

224. We marked all entrances or possible entrances off Houston Plaza to the buildings around it: to Irvine Auditorium, Houston Hall—the original student union, now too small—College Hall, and Williams Hall. With a little reworking of circulation, we could bring a great deal of movement into the area. We felt this should be the location of the new student center. Reuse Houston Hall, occupy spaces off every doorway on Houston Plaza, and you'll have a student center precinct.

225. The Perelman Quad on Wynn Commons. It contains study halls on the main floor of Houston Hall and throughout the precinct, and there are activity areas of different types to handle different needs. There is a big basement cafeteria under the Commons as well as several coffee shops at the Commons level, including one in Irvine, where the auditorium has been adapted and preserved and a small performance area added. These are all part of the new campus center.

THE STREET THROUGH THE BUILDING

Frist Campus Center at Princeton University, 1996–2000

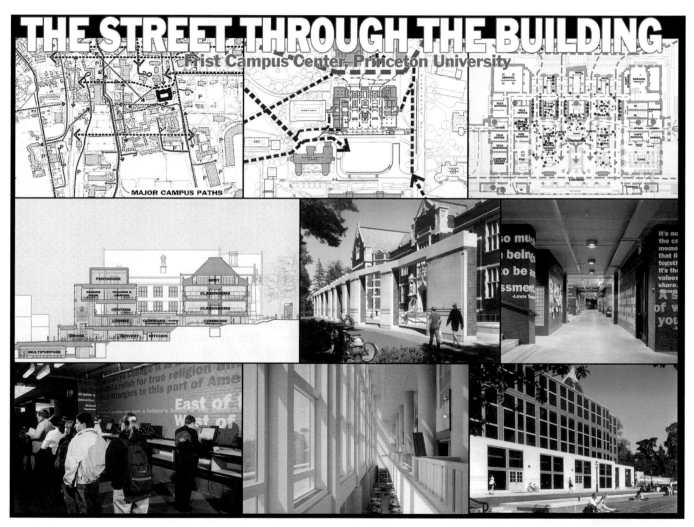

226. At Frist Hall, we converted a staid classroom building into an expansive campus center. Although it may not seem to be, this existing building is located centrally on campus. Pedestrian circulation running beside the building is pulled into and through it, to a big new entity at its center. The "streets" through the building are narrow, like medieval alleys, and are lined with stores and with communication-graffiti. The streets lead to a large commons area at the back, where a very big window lights several floors of activity.

OVERLAYING PATTERNS

University of Michigan Master Plan and a Life Sciences Complex,
1997–2004

Via these maps we took a series of analytic cross-cuts through the data,
then recombined some variables to see what we could learn.

227. The University of Michigan, as it started . . .

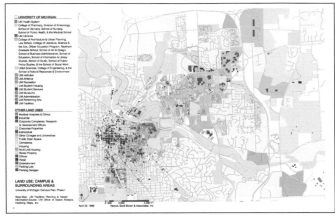

228. . . . and as it grew to be a 3,000 acre campus that stalks across the city of Ann Arbor. The main campus and downtown sit cheek by jowl. Starting in 1997, as the university's planners, we mapped the activities of town and gown together to try to understand their shared patterns. The CBD and the main campus look like two cells in mitosis.

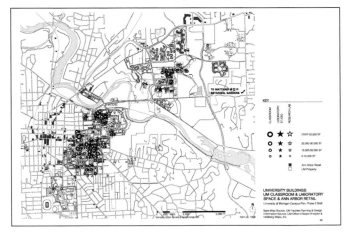

231. More UM patterns. We disaggregated the land-use map into its various components. This map shows the sciences crossing the campuses.

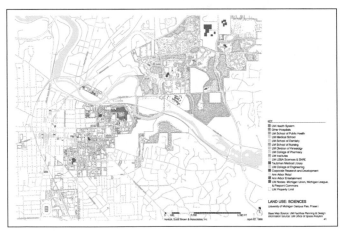

232. Classrooms, studios, and labs are shown by size and juxtaposed with commercial uses to illustrate the relationship between them.

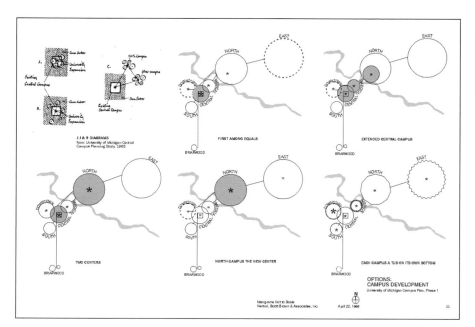

230. We showed how the university has expanded and discussed its options for the future.

229. The University of Michigan's north, medical, and main campuses.

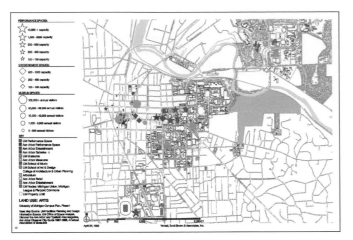

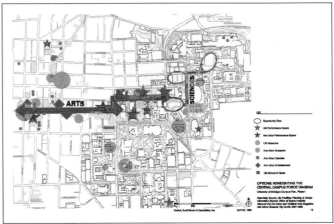

233, 234. The distribution of arts, performing arts, and museums. The linear pattern of arts facilities, stretching from the campus into the town, is reminiscent of the Zipf graph discussed above. We recommended there be a focus on the arts within an axis running east-west from town to gown, then suggested several sites, near the famous UM Diag but accessible to the medical center, that would be suitable for laboratory buildings. At the Palmer Drive site, life sciences can link with academic sciences on the main campus and with research in the medical school.

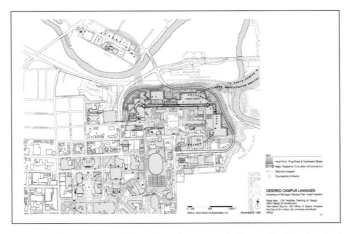

235. There is a need to go from the main campus to the medical center—but this involves crossing a busy state highway. The Palmer Drive site lies across the line of communication between the two.

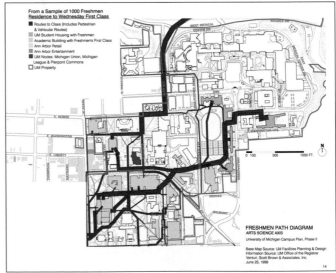

236. Student circulation from residences to classes passes near but not through the site.

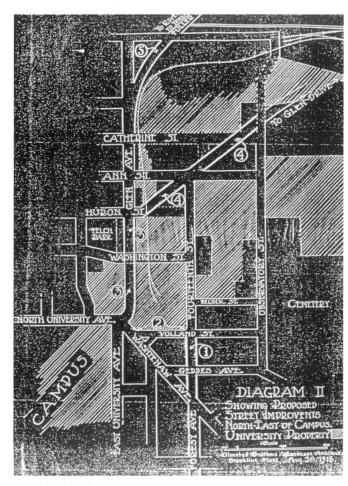

237. In 1916 Olmstead discerned the same problem we did—that parts of the campus were not linked.

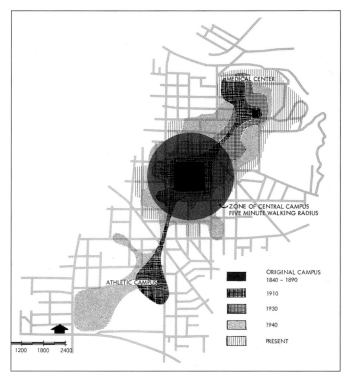

ORIGINAL CAMPUS
1840 - 1890

1910

1930

1940

PRESENT

238. In 1963 Johnson, Johnson & Roy showed an ectoplasm-like pattern making the needed linkage, but it wasn't clear at that time how this should be accomplished.

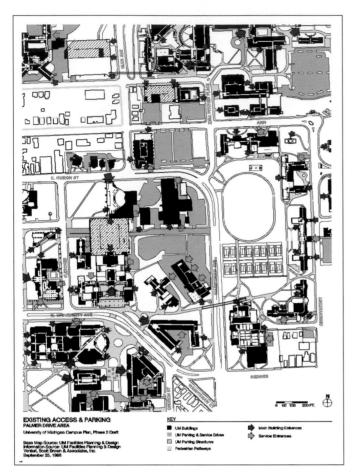

EXISTING ACCESS & PARKING
PALMER DRIVE AREA
University of Michigan Campus Plan, Phase 2 Draft

Base Map Source: UM Facilities Planning & Design
Information Source: UM Facilities Planning & Design
Venturi, Scott Brown & Associates, Inc.
September 25, 1998

KEY
■ UM Buildings
▧ UM Parking & Service Drives
▨ UM Parking Structures
☐ Pedestrian Pathways
► Main Building Entrances
► Service Entrances

N
0 50 100   200 FT.

239, 240. We made our Nolli map for UM as we do for every campus. The pink is pedestrian ways; gray is parking lots—something Nolli did not have to contend with. The site is a big parking lot in what was once a lake. The state highway runs alongside it. We noticed that a bridge across the highway south of the site needed no hump because it follows the lake edge. Then, from a topographical analysis we determined that a walkway could span the lake diagonally from edge to edge, cross the Palmer Drive site and the road, link the main and the medical campuses, and stay at the same level all the way across. Above the bridge could be academic and research buildings; below it, parking.

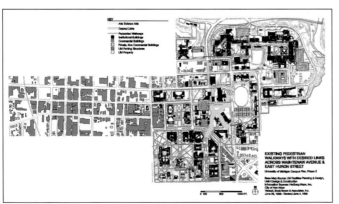

KEY
Arts Science Arts
Desired Links
Pedestrian Walkways
Institutional Buildings
Commercial Buildings
Private, Non Commercial Buildings
UM Parking Structures
UM Property

EXISTING PEDESTRIAN
WALKWAYS WITH DESIRED LINKS
ACROSS WASHTENAW AVENUE &
EAST HURON STREET
University of Michigan Campus Plan, Phase 2

Base Map Source: UM Facilities Planning & Design,
UM Design & Construction
Information Source: Hedberg Maps, Inc.,
City of Ann Arbor
Venturi, Scott Brown & Associates, Inc.
June 25, 1998 - Revised June 4, 1999

0 100   500   1000 FT.

MAJOR PEDESTRIAN ACCESS TO PALMER DRIVE & ZINA PITCHER COMPLEXES
WALKWAY LEVEL
University of Michigan Campus Plan, Phase 2 Draft

Base Map Source: UM Facilities Planning & Design
Venturi, Scott Brown & Associates, Inc.
May 20, 1999

N
☐ Main Entrances
○ Service Entrances
◌ Pedestrian Access

241, 242. Borrowing from the transportation planners, we drew "desire lines" across the lake between academic sciences and medical sciences and between arts and sciences. Then we designed our buildings around the desire lines. The complex includes the Life Sciences Institute laboratory, an undergraduate sciences building, and a commons building. Alongside these are a bridge, various open spaces, and several walkways. Below the walkway level is structured parking for 960 cars.

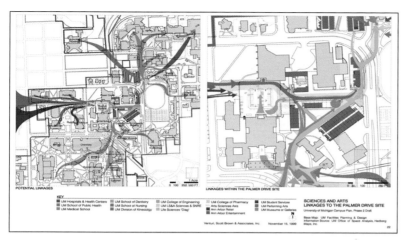

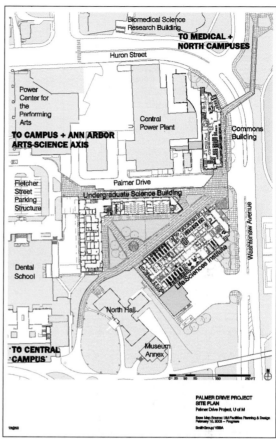

243, 244. An aim of the project was to support interdisciplinary communication by enhancing linkage within the plan. Linkage is via the Arts and Sciences Axis and the Life Sciences Diag. The place where the two meet we call the Meeting of Minds. As you go by the Commons on your way to the medical center, you may see a friend in the café and stop for a chat; then, where will the Nobel Prize be gestated, at the lab bench or over coffee?

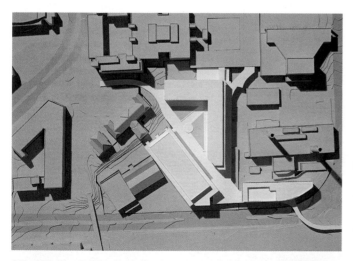

245, 246. The buildings are simple and generic. The pedestrian walkways and open spaces, which form the public sector, are complex and are intended to be like the streets and spaces of a medieval town—informal and not too wide. There are "streets" through the buildings, too, to serve local communities. These internal circulation systems connect to the outdoor walkways at the third-floor level.

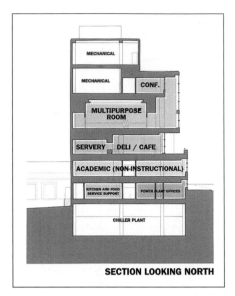

MECHANICAL

MECHANICAL | CONF.

MULTIPURPOSE ROOM

SERVERY | DELI / CAFE

ACADEMIC (NON-INSTRUCTIONAL)

KITCHEN AND FOOD SERVICE SUPPORT | POWER PLANT OFFICES

CHILLER PLANT

SECTION LOOKING NORTH

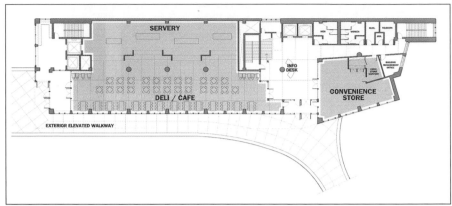

SERVERY

DELI / CAFE

INFO DESK

CONVENIENCE STORE

EXTERIOR ELEVATED WALKWAY

247, 248. Land-use planning inside the commons building: the deli and café are at the walkway level, the store is at the exterior corner where stores should be and by the entrance, where most people will pass. People will come together for various purposes throughout this building. We hope its spaces will be shared by students, scientists, medical researchers, people from the performing arts facilities, and others going between the main and medical campuses.

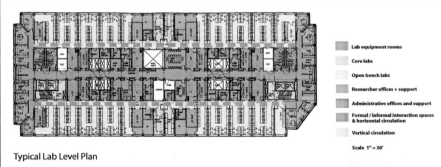

Lab equipment rooms

Core labs

Open bench labs

Researcher offices + support

Administrative offices and support

Formal / informal interaction spaces & horizontal circulation

Vertical circulation

Scale 1" = 30'

Typical Lab Level Plan

249. Within the life sciences laboratory building, "streets" run from labs and offices to stairs and elevators, passing near interaction spaces, where people can get coffee, see a different view, change their focal length, think, chat, and draw together on the white board—more urban planning inside.

250. The Life Sciences Institute and the Commons Building in construction.

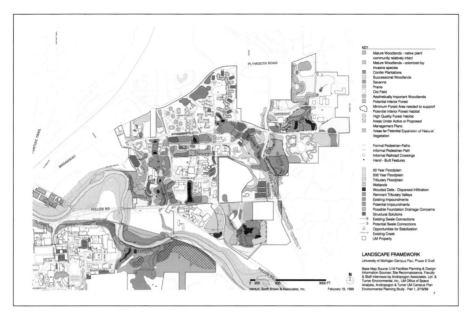

251. Environmental framework planning is another system-wide discipline that conditions our design. The map analyzes environmental factors that should influence planning and design on the UM North Campus.

In this discussion, we have moved from planning analyses of patterns (derived mostly from urban economic and transportation systems) to the planning of buildings using similar principles. These principles represent an extension of architectural ideas of "function" into a wider geographical and intellectual territory. They offer one further layer of ideas to add to the many that architects now bring to design. To me, they have the advantage of being concrete, understandable, and fairly easily adaptable to architecture, yet also beautiful, provocative, even a little mystical.

— 7 —
The Redefinition of Functionalism

What is the function of a table?
Bob and I are dour functionalists. We see the Modern Movement's belief in functionalism as one of its glories. While Postmodern and Neomodern architects have departed from early Modern doctrines on function, we have remained functionalists for both moral and aesthetic reasons. But if the function of even as simple an object as a table fights definition, how much more difficult can the definition be in architecture? And the problem is exacerbated when time and society are included. This chapter is a call to reassess our views on how buildings function, should function, or can be seen as functioning.

Various definitions of functionalism
Le Corbusier recommended that architecture students examine ship docks, the storage provisions in train kitchens, and the rear facades of buildings, to see true functionalism at work. The London architect Ernö Goldfinger, my employer for six difficult months, once yelled at me, "You say you're a functionalist—*this* is functionalism!" He was referring to how the plumbing worked in a building, and that *is* an aspect of functionalism.

But how do you define the function of a building that has housed ranges of activities over some hundreds of years? How "functional" is it to plan for the first users (for the client's program or brief) and not give thought to how it may adapt to generations of users in the unforeseeable future? We should consider widening our definition of function beyond Le Corbusier's and Goldfinger's architectural equivalents of time-and-motion studies.

The palazzo was essentially a loft that could accommodate these changes and, over a span of four hundred years, its form remained essentially the same. The history of its development can be described largely through the stylistic change in the decoration of its façades.[1] Something similar applies to college halls and to various urban building types. Our

What is the function of a table?

252, 253. I may work at it or read at it.

258, 259. It can symbolize power or spiritual relationships.

254, 255. Children can convert it to a boat or a house.

256, 257. I may dance on it or drink myself under it.

260. And a hundred years later it may be an antique.

261, 262. In some residential quarters of Venice, houses have been lived in since the twelfth century. During this time, their structures may have remained more or less intact, but plumbing has been changed, spaces and furnishings altered numerous times, and the way of life within them shifted again and again. Many historic building types no longer serve their original purposes. Italian Renaissance palazzos, once dynastic abodes that were also warehouses and stores, have been converted to apartments, museums and other institutions, or government agencies.

office, for example, is in an industrial loft building that started as a flatted warehouse or factory, gives signs of having served at one time as a roller-skating rink, and now provides the good lighting, high ceilings, and uninterrupted floor space we need for the practice of architecture.

Change of this kind over time tends to obscure the clarity of the relationship that is conveyed in the notion that form follows function. What does it do to the triad firmness, commodity, and delight:

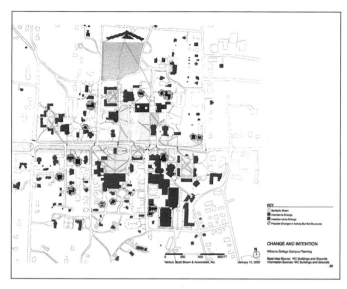

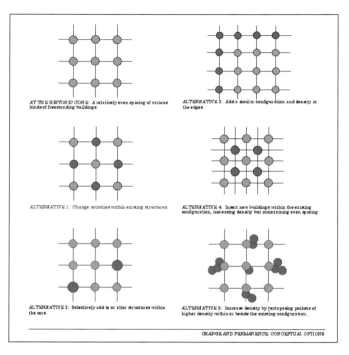

263, 264. Change in buildings and cities can concern their structures, their activities, or both. How should the fact that activities frequently change within existing structures affect the definition of function?

- as formulated by Vitruvius?
  (**F**irmness + **C**ommodity + **D**elight = **A**rchitecture)
- by Gropius?
  (**F**irmness + **C**ommodity = **D**elight)
- and in Robert Venturi's juxtaposition of the two?

Definitions from other fields

It could be instructive to consider how "function" is defined by different disciplines, from biology, where it concerns the workings of life systems, to mathematics, where it describes the character and operations of numerical abstractions. A mathematical expression of the views of Vitruvius and Gropius might be:

$$\text{Vitruvius: } \mathbf{A} = f(\mathbf{F},\mathbf{C},\mathbf{D})$$
$$\text{Gropius: } \mathbf{D} = f(\mathbf{F},\mathbf{C})$$

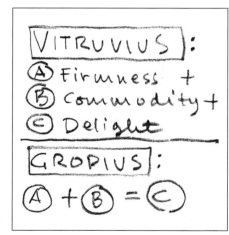

265.

An overview of the possibilities of the term by the sociologist Robert Merton was required reading in Herbert Gans's course on urban sociology.[2] Through this article I learned the clumsy but useful word *dysfunctional* and pondered Merton's caveat that seemingly dysfunctional phenomena must be functional for someone, otherwise they wouldn't exist; the questions being, "For whom?" and "Why?"

Gans related Merton's observations to urbanism and to a critique of architecture. He advised that before we define conditions we dislike— for example, urban sprawl—as pathological, we try to understand why they exist and who benefits from them. This brought up one more aspect of the architectural view of functionalism: its subjectivity; and a further criticism of the practice of architects: they seldom ask, "Who should define function?"

I began to consider how such questions could guide a critical appraisal of the idea of function in architecture, and of the processes of defining it in the program. What should be the basis for the definitions? Part could be cultural. I remember a design made at the AA for a judge's house in Chandigarh by an architecture student from Nepal. In his plan, the guest room was reached via the kitchen. What greater hospitality, he asked, could be offered guests than to be able to refresh themselves at will?

Architectural function should perhaps be defined through a political process to assure the representation of those being planned for. The Penn social planners felt that architects in urban design and housing were over-ready to assign functions and set out required functional relationships without canvassing the people concerned. They claimed that when we architects plan for client groups that we can't or don't meet— future tenants of public housing, for example—we decide they will want what we want. Even the codes and legal standards for building are derived, the planners alleged, from some group's value judgments on what is good.

In the end, users assign their own programmatic interpretations to the buildings and spaces they occupy, doing so, as the architect does, sub-jectively and self-referentially. I heard no sophisticated social scientist demand that architects be "value free"; indeed our subjectivity was seen as a potentially valuable contribution to the process, as long as we were aware of it and able to set it alongside other, more outwardly-oriented, tools for defining function.

The social planners may have missed methods that exist within archi-tecture for broadening the definition of function or for supplementing its subjectivity. One method is to employ professional programmers to research the needs of the institution and its users. As well, architects have learned, for some purposes, to step back from a listing of specific rooms for single functions—living room, bedroom, classroom, lab—to more general descriptions. Mies van der Rohe's "generalized" spaces and Louis Kahn's "master" and "servant" spaces fit this category. Or we can place urban building types along a spectrum of themes—the row house; the warehouse and industrial loft; the office building; the store; latter-day reformulations of all these in suburbia; and, recently, the revived traditional themes of the "New Urbanism."

Architects can also consider how patterns of activities and structures fall out of alignment with each other as urban areas undergo change. The urbanist's view of these shifting relationships is at odds with the architect's. In the design of individual buildings, architects seek a close fit between program and spaces. They are seldom trained to consider how future generations may change the uses of the building and, because such thinking drives up costs, they may not have the luxury of doing so.

Then there is the public–private formulation. This cuts across building types, separating governmental and institutional buildings from private ones. But it can define parts within a building too. In every house and institutional building there is a gradation from public to pri-vate. And within the public there is also the civic. A beach is public. People go there to use a public good, but they stay in their own groups,

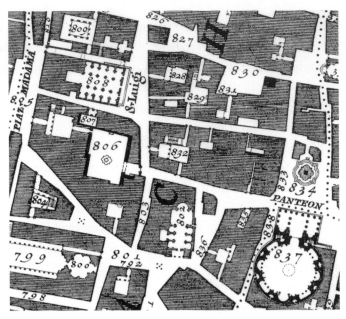

266. Beachgoers seem spread, as if by some mathematical law, as far from others as possible within the available space.
267. Nolli's depiction of the public sector (or much of it) of Rome has served as a model for us for analyzing public and private spaces, in both planning and architecture.

each family an island on its mats and towels. The boardwalk, however, is civic. People walk it to see and be seen, and in City Hall or Symphony Hall we are part of a community, of the city, or perhaps the world.

Other categories useful for broadening our view of function include: temporary to permanent, involving sequential change over time; functional relationships within and among buildings, involving the concept of linkage; and, at a less tangible level, psychological, symbolic, and communicative functions.

Function, functional relationships, and linkage

The architectural design process initiates with a list of activities users intend to engage in and a schedule of accommodations—a program—to house them. This is accompanied by guidelines on how the activities must be related to fulfill the purposes of building users. The notion of linkage—between activities within a building, between buildings, and between the activities of the city—augments the idea of functional relation. The spaces, their relationships, and the means of connecting them

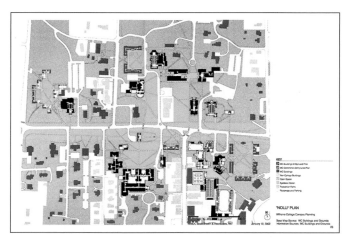

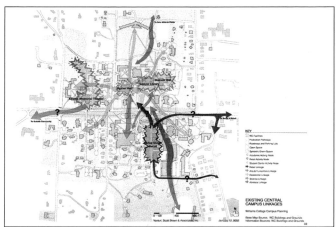

268. Here we have mapped the campus buildings of Williams College, as Nolli did the churches of Rome, by their poché. This allows us to show public spaces and corridors inside buildings linked to public spaces of the campus, and particularly to pathways that lead from outdoor spaces to those inside buildings. These are mapped as a linked network in the central sector of the campus.

269. This map shows linkage between activities in various buildings on the Williams campus. The linkage diagram suggests that change planned for one part of the network—an addition of a new building or a new wing—calls for change in another, for example redirecting or adding to pathways and circulation systems.

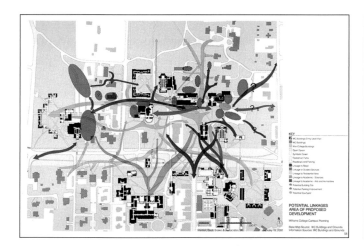

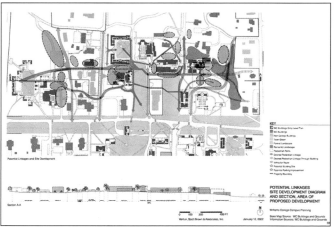

270. We map proposals that have been made for additional building at the center of the campus and develop an overlay of old and new linkage needs that will result from the introduction of three large projects at the center of the campus.

271. Based on the future linkage requirements, we suggest a new pathway system, running east-west just north of the central campus, to connect the new projects to one another and the larger environment.

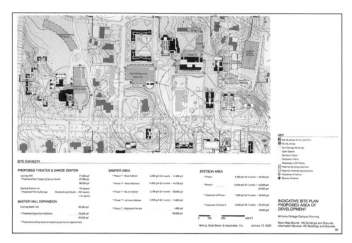

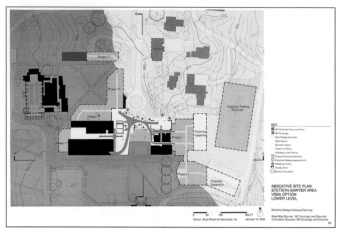

SITE CAPACITY

PROPOSED THEATER & DANCE CENTER

BAXTER HALL EXPANSION

SAWYER AREA

STETSON AREA

INDICATIVE SITE PLAN
PROPOSED AREA OF
DEVELOPMENT

INDICATIVE SITE PLAN
STETSON-SAWYER AREA
VSBA OPTION
LOWER LEVEL

272, 273. We examined the college's building intentions in greater detail and suggested how programmed elements could be arranged to provide the connections between the humanities offices, library, and classrooms desired by the faculty. We suggested these might be tied together by exploiting level changes on the site and by locating new classrooms and a coffee shop under the plaza between the library and the major humanities building. Well lit on one side, thanks to the change in level, and with good access from both buildings, this area could become the meeting place the faculty called for.

generate the major anatomy of the design—*of course*, the experienced architect considers, along with these, structure, mechanical and environmental systems, a host of theories and philosophies, the architectural character the client is hoping to achieve, and a vocabulary of favorite things.

Does form follow function?

The Van Nelle Factory epitomizes the form-follows-function doctrine. Built near Rotterdam for packaging coffee, tea, and tobacco, it was a flatted factory, where the processes moved from the top floor downward and across the road via chutes flanked by a tall industrial chimney. Strong supporting columns designed to hold heavy loads are visible within the building through its glass and steel curtain walls. Vertical and horizontal circulation elements and administrative offices read clearly on its façade, and above all sits the directors' lounge, a circular space of steel and glass, with a 360-degree view of the surrounding landscape.

What a challenge these architects must have sensed, "grasping the

274. The Van Nelle Factory, Rotterdam, 1925 to 1931.

imperatives of modern industry" and reasoning them through to a design. This must have been how they saw it—and all in the interest of packaging products! There was no symbolism here, they would have said, and no aesthetics. (I am guessing. I never met J. Brinkman and L. V. van der Vlugt, the architects, but I was in the building.) Every detail is grounded in the idea of a new industrial era, and the results are, for me, one of the most beautiful buildings in the world—but a demonstration, too, of how a formal vocabulary, unadmitted, can govern every inch of the design. Was any functional need slighted by the perhaps unconscious aesthetic aim? You would have to ask the clients and users of the building. Are artists able to deceive themselves as to their motives? Yes, in many fields. Does this matter? Sometimes, when the needs of users go unmet or when a better solution could have been found by carefully following the requirements. These are poignant thoughts in view of the great beauty of the building.

How did it survive change over time? I imagined that in Holland, as in the United States, flatted factories are no longer practical. Did slavish attention to functional needs, real or imagined, prevent the Van Nelle factory from having other uses later? An email and a website uncovered the fact that it is now a "collective building," containing design offices, with emphasis on new media and IT, and offering various (communal?) facilities including exhibition space.[3] Probably its heavy columns and glass walls were better suited to the light and space needs of design studios than to regular office cubicles, but we can surmise that among its most endearing features to its new users were its looks. These may have saved it from unsympathetic reuse. Were its looks part of its "function"? Does this put the lie to the form-follows-function philosophy?

Where is A?
Robert Venturi, in setting Gropius against Vitruvius, in effect asked, if $D = F + C$ then where is A?[4] The early Modernists and the Brutalists following them scorned Architecture with a capital A. To them, it was an eclectic encrustation that belonged with the nineteenth-century

"Battle of the Styles" and should be scraped off. The less talked about Art in architecture the better, they felt. Beauty, having had its name taken in vain, should no longer be discussed but should be achieved, if at all, by indirection, as a resultant. But Van Nelle shows what secret store they set by it, and much of *Learning from Las Vegas* was spent analyzing the self-deception of the later Moderns as they proclaimed "truth to function and structure" but designed unadmitted decoration.

Our Duck and Decorated Shed arose from this analysis. For most buildings we recommend the Decorated Shed. We see the shed component as following early Modern principles. It does its job, achieves beauty by indirection, and is not at first noticed as beautiful (we call it "second glance architecture"). Then a limited spattering of quite conscious "beauty" (delight, decoration, symbolism, iconography, communication—it takes many forms) can be applied, where it counts.

I have suggested that, as in Van Nelle, a building's aesthetic quality may be part of its function. But what about the political question, "Who decides what is beautiful?" This can lead to hellholes for both democracy and designers.

Form follows forces

In Chapter 6, I considered how an economy formed patterns of settlement on the land. To illustrate how economic forces affect form, I used the Zulu kraal and the plan of Philadelphia. These showed the difference between a subsistence economy and one based on trade. Philadelphia is subtended by its connectedness in all directions, nationally and locally. Around the kraal there are no roads. Cow paths lead to the water and a footpath goes off into the hills. The settlement is organized for families and livestock, and for scratching a living from the soil. (In fact, subsistence is not attainable and the economy of the unit depends in part on labor in a distant trading society.)

In the "Form, Forces, and Function" studios I ran at Penn and UCLA in the 1960s, we tried to understand to what extent urban form was determined by the economy, but also by the technology available to the society, particularly the technology of movement. We considered social and demographic factors and environmental and geographic determinants that must be understood at both macro and micro scales. We asked how changes in form might emerge as a result of changes in forces. Suburbia, its social and economic causes and the role of the automobile in its development, held our attention then and would do so now, but today we would discuss as well how patterns of living, working, leisure, education, commerce, and production are evolving in relation to computer-generated changes in the technology of communication and in response to global economic and social forces.

Form accommodates function

If the association of form and function cannot be reduced to a simple Modernist mantra, if Le Corbusier's train kitchen illuminates the relation less well than we had hoped, are there nevertheless other useful metaphors? We propose a glove and a mitten.

The glove is shaped to hold each finger, and gloves are graded by size. The mitten limits hand movement to grasping, but it allows wiggle room on the inside and can fit a wide range of hand sizes. Should buildings be designed as mittens rather than gloves, to meet generic rather than specific definitions of function? In a mitten-building, some program elements of today may sit a little less well, but these are likely to change even before the building is constructed. In many projects, sacrificing some adherence to the specifics of present programs may be worthwhile for the flexibility this offers the future.

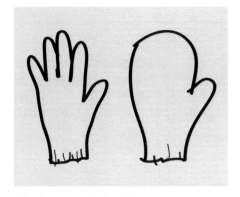

275. The glove and the mitten.

Form accommodates change

Kevin Lynch in an article on change and adaptability suggested several ways of designing buildings and urban areas to allow them to adapt over time.[5] These included the expensive option of providing extra space, but he suggested, as well, measures for separating systems so that structural and mechanical elements, for example, could change without interrupting the activities they were serving. Regular and generous column bays, structures strong enough to take a range of uses, and lighting systems that allowed for a variety of activities were part of the recommendation.

Lynch felt buildings planned for change per se had a better chance of satisfying over their lifetime than those based on predictions of specific changes to come. He recommended planning for the unpredictable.

Unfortunately most means of planning for change—articulation, separation and allowing extra space—are expensive. An alternative used for low-cost structures is to plan in advance to demolish and build again. Retail commercial buildings, which may need regular face-lifts in any case because customers tire easily of their looks, tend to have cheap façades that can be easily replaced. But civic and institutional uses are better served by the principle that the building will mellow with age and accommodate many different purposes through its commodiousness—by the mitten rather than the glove.

Seeking the generic
What is the equivalent of the mitten in architecture?

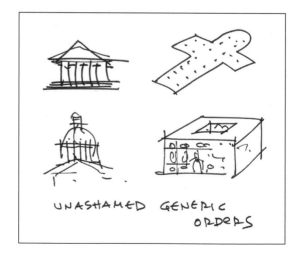

UNASHAMED GENERIC ORDERS

276. Building forms that have accommodated ranges of functions over time include the basilica, adapted from the law courts of ancient Rome to all manner of churches, over more than two thousand years; the loft building; and the palazzo. Home now to diverse institutions or converted to an apartment building, the palazzo is also the progenitor of the "palazzetto," a modern Roman apartment building type.

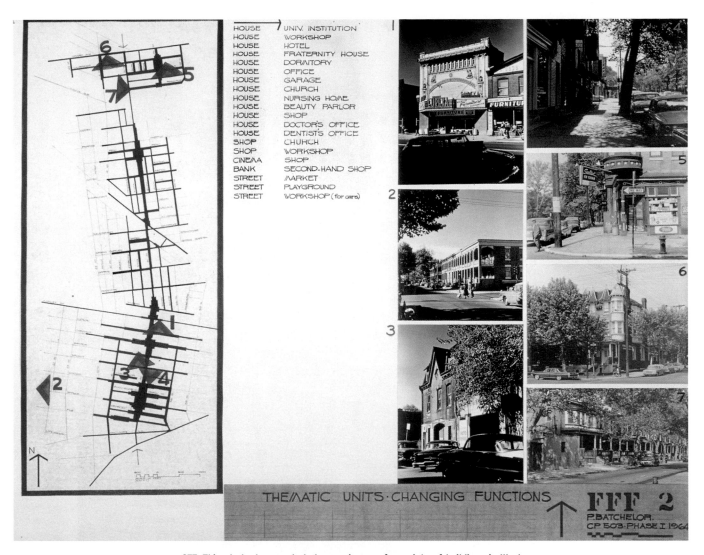

HOUSE → UNIV. INSTITUTION
HOUSE → WORKSHOP
HOUSE → HOTEL
HOUSE → FRATERNITY HOUSE
HOUSE → DORMITORY
HOUSE → OFFICE
HOUSE → GARAGE
HOUSE → CHURCH
HOUSE → NURSING HOME
HOUSE → BEAUTY PARLOR
HOUSE → SHOP
HOUSE → DOCTOR'S OFFICE
HOUSE → DENTIST'S OFFICE
SHOP → CHURCH
SHOP → WORKSHOP
CINEMA → SHOP
BANK → SECOND-HAND SHOP
STREET → MARKET
STREET → PLAYGROUND
STREET → WORKSHOP (for cars)

THEMATIC UNITS · CHANGING FUNCTIONS

FFF 2
P. BATCHELOR.
CP 503 · PHASE I 1964

277. This study documented changes in use of a variety of buildings in West Philadelphia over perhaps half a century—from cinema to store, store to church, and house to institution, hotel, shop, church, nursing home, offices, and on and on.

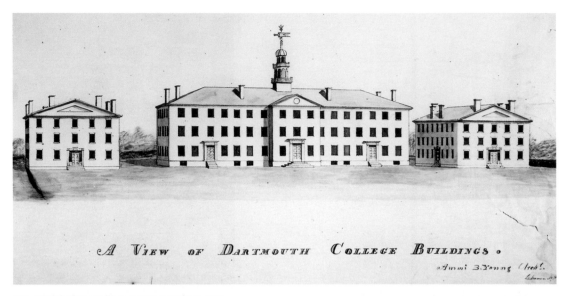

A VIEW OF DARTMOUTH COLLEGE BUILDINGS.

278. "Old College Hall" on many American campuses is like a loft building. Over time, it has contained classrooms, dormitories, and administrative offices.

279. The college lab building, with its regular, generous bays and large windows, can support sequences of uses. As its systems become outmoded for today's sciences, it can be adapted to lower-tech scientific and teaching uses.

GENERIC DESIGN FOR FLEXIBILITY

Similar lab-window relationship at UPenn's Clinical Research Building

GOLDSCHMIED

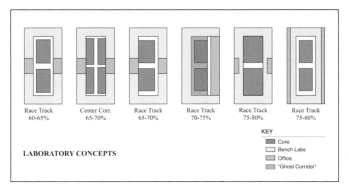

| Race Track 60-65% | Center Corr. 65-70% | Race Track 65-70% | Race Track 70-75% | Race Track 75-80% | Race Track 75-80% |

KEY
- Core
- Bench Labs
- Office
- "Ghost Corridor"

LABORATORY CONCEPTS

280. Gonda (Goldschmied) Neuroscience and Genetics Research Center, UCLA, 1998. Our life science research labs are slab buildings whose generous widths can accommodate the layouts the sciences require, and whose rhythms of structure and lighting are determined by lab-bench dimensions. At the ends of the building, beyond the structured lab spaces, can be unique places, less generic, less adaptable, that serve as resting and social areas. Located on main routes near vertical circulation elements, these can take the shapes of meeting and conviviality.

281. The amount of support space needed at the centers of lab floors is increasing exponentially in the life sciences today and is an important consideration in lab design. Circulation systems are designed according to the scientists' views on the relation between lab, office, and support space.

Building Typologies and Thematic Units

Apart from the lab, what are our society's building themes, equivalent to the basilica, palazzo, and loft? Imagine a model train set, placed within its model landscape. What buildings would be in the toy train town? How would the schoolhouse, fire station, town hall, bank, and post office look? (Forget, for the moment, whether we're in Maine or New Mexico, or the tendency of archetypes to look old-fashioned.) What new uses should join this hierarchy? A Starbucks?

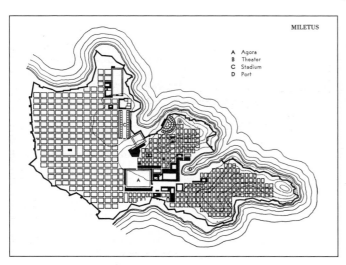

282. In the plan of Miletus the various building themes stand out clearly. There are several different residential areas and a public sector that contains an amphitheater and an agora.

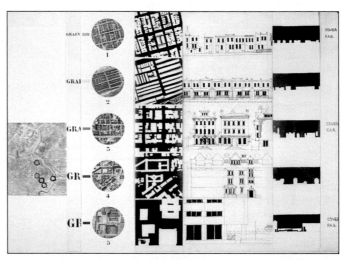

283. In this West Philadelphia study, building themes are analyzed via aerial photographs, plans, sections, and elevations.

In both cities the generic grid ties the elements to one another and to the topography. There is a book to be written on how the urban grid plan can accommodate diverse activities, allow for change, become a plaid when the volume of transportation increases, adapt to topography and, in the process, become unique yet remain generic.[6]

284. Louis Kahn, searching for generic themes for his dormitory building at Bryn Mawr, seems to be building a small city. The units bear a likeness to row houses in Philadelphia. He organizes them to form three "kraals" within the building. As fascinating as his themes and typologies is Kahn's method of searching for form. The drawings become clearer and the outlines more firm, as his voyage of discovery progresses.

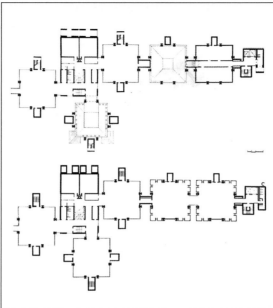

285. Kahn arrived at a typology for his Richards Medical Lab building through his famous formulation of master and servant spaces. These bear a family resemblance to the "generalized" space of Mies van der Rohe, but Kahn has separated structural elements, stairs, and service spaces and placed them beyond the envelope of the general space. It's ironic that this system, devised for functional accommodation, should have turned out to be difficult for scientists to work in. The dimensions of the master spaces were unsuitable for lab uses and the circulation through the centers of the units was inconvenient. They might have made good architecture studios—"If you architects like them, take them," the biologists suggested sarcastically. In his next lab, at the Salk Center, Kahn got it right.

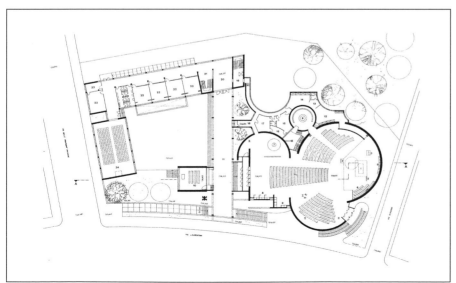

286. In his Church of San Gregorio Barbarigo, Giuseppe Vaccaro also sought typologies. He grew them out of the fan shape of seats in the sanctuary. The sanctuary and community spaces are linked by a breezeway, a shared unique space.

The lab and the church, although relatively small, each contain a hierarchy of building themes. Kahn did not consider setting his generic units against something other than servant spaces—against the unique spaces of the public sector. Even his main entrance is a "master" space left open. The inclusion of unique spaces would have caused a reversal in Kahn's schema: the main circulation spaces, through their uses and connections, would have become part of the public sector, foreground rather background. They would have been civic. Kahn does form such a civic sector in the three interconnected centers of the Bryn Mawr dormitories; and in Vaccaro's church the combination of the generic fan components, the breezeway, and a cross at the main entrance constitutes the civic portion of the complex.

In museums, where the major circulation space must handle crowds, ours takes on the bulbous, wormlike shape of crowd movement. Off it are the generic, adaptable spaces that hold the changeable functions of the building. The "master" space becomes background. Frank Lloyd Wright's Guggenheim Museum, at the other extreme, is almost all public sector, yet it too involves a surprising reversal. It's a monument formed by access corridors, by servant spaces wound up to make one wonderful, unique whole—helical spring as museum. There's no generic here. The building is not adaptable and barely accommodates its own museum functions. The only reuse I could imagine for it would be as a parking structure for motor scooters.

Streets as typologies

Lou Kahn evolved a typology of streets, which he likened to waterways, and eventuallly he addded an extra category—the street within the building.

Learning from Kahn, Crane, and transportation planning, we have taken this internal street, tied it to external pathways that leadd to the building, and made it the spine of the public sector of our buildings.

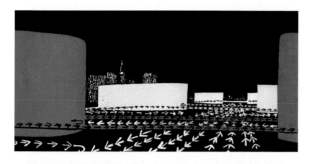

287. Lou Kahn's Philadelphia traffic studies.

288. VSBA's "Street through the building."

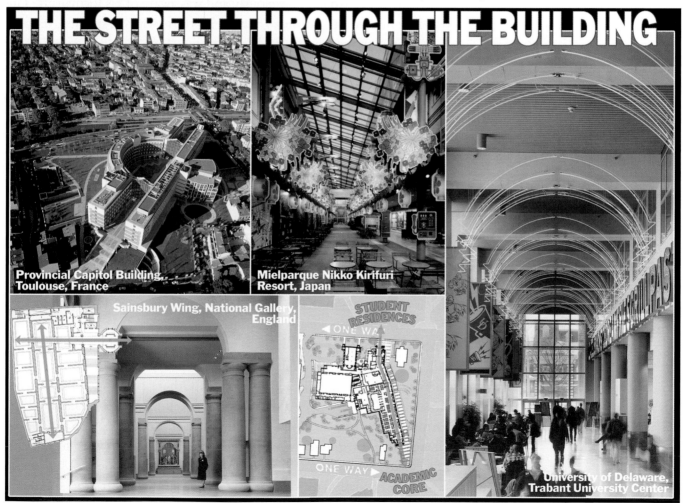

THE STREET THROUGH THE BUILDING

Provincial Capitol Building, Toulouse, France

Mielparque Nikko Kirifuri Resort, Japan

Sainsbury Wing, National Gallery, England

University of Delaware, Trabant University Center

Does form follow form?

Once we loosen the constraints of "form follows function," the form–function equation encounters various challenges.

In the Furness Building at the University of Pennsylvania, the borrowings from historical architecture range from the Scottish highlands to the Grand Canal. Historical rules are abrogated and formal vocabularies blended, as the elements are lifted, shifted, and placed to suit the internal needs of the building. But Frank Furness, unlike the architects of the Van Nelle factory, borrowed consciously and was aware of his formalism. The building housed the Furness Library. In 1891, when it opened, its plan represented an innovation in library science. One hundred years later it accepted the electronic revolution extremely well. Its diversity of spaces accommodated the late twentieth-century computer needs of the Fisher Fine Arts Library, and its light and spaciousness made it a study hall of choice for students far from the disciplines it served. Library functions were not scanted as a result of the architect's formal preoccupations.

Does function follow form?

However, the word "formalism" is often used with the words "flashy" or "superficial" to suggest that attention to form is irresponsible. The possibility that function may follow rather than dictate form, or that function might be winkled into a preconceived form, is looked upon as bad. Yet the Furness Building shows that function is not necessarily constrained as a result of idiosyncratic form or through interest in formal precedents.

Does form evoke function?

The Furness Building's unique shapes give people ideas for its use. Some spaces would be wonderful for a party. Others by happy accident are suitable for architecture studios. This is a building much in demand. Its form does not exactly follow its function, but it does adapt to functional change. Its form derives from earlier form. Its functions both follow and are evoked by its form. Are its form and function one? This was a favorite formulation of Matthew Nowicki, but I think it's too simple.

289, 290. The Furness Building, University of Pennsylvania.

Is communication a function?

If the concept of function can be broadened to include everything we have discussed above, then certainly communication—architecture used as language—can be considered an aspect of function, and indeed Part I of this book has been devoted to it.

Architecture's communicative function was disregarded throughout the first half of the twentieth century. During the 1950s, Bob and I independently developed a strong interest in it. In the mid 1960s we looked for a site where we could study architectural communication somewhat separately from architecture's other functions and away from complex urban patterns that would make the communication systems less clear. We found it in the Nevada desert on the Las Vegas Strip.

The idea of the building as a shed with communication on it has influenced all our work but particularly our civic buildings. The changeable nature of LED permits quick shifts in communication, almost as events happen. Its electronic banners have the same immediacy as flags or flowers. They stand in contrast to the masonry of the buildings, much as the blossoms on the altar stood against the thousand-year-old temple, and they permit an immediacy and variability of urban communication that would astound architectural propagandists of earlier eras, who incised their messages in stone.

A question for the future might be whether architects will be prepared to surrender the creative tasks of symbolic communication via architecture to the graphic artists who design the LED messages. Will we (or our clients) want this major element of the building to be expressed through a medium that is innately not subject to control? Will we abrogate, to this extent, our own expressive and decorative needs—needs that eventually led us away from the abstractions of Modernism? Will designing the shed and the frame that holds the decoration be enough for us?

291, 292. Symbol in
space before form in
space.

It's not about space:
it's about communication

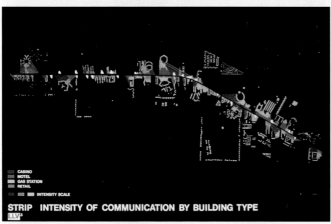

STRIP INTENSITY OF COMMUNICATION BY BUILDING TYPE

CASINO
MOTEL
GAS STATION
RETAIL
INTENSITY SCALE

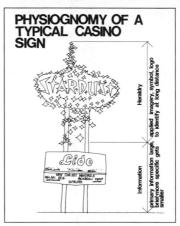

PHYSIOGNOMY OF A TYPICAL CASINO SIGN

293, 294, 295, 296, 297, 298.
The Las Vegas Strip circa 1968.

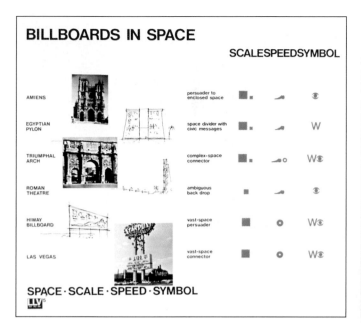

BILLBOARDS IN SPACE

SCALESPEEDSYMBOL

AMIENS	persuader to enclosed space			
EGYPTIAN PYLON	space divider with civic messages			W
TRIUMPHAL ARCH	complex-space connector			W
ROMAN THEATRE	ambiguous back drop			
HIWAY BILLBOARD	vast-space persuader			W
LAS VEGAS	vast-space connector			W

SPACE · SCALE · SPEED · SYMBOL

299, 300. How architecture and signs combined to send messages to people riding the Strip became a point of departure for our investigation into latter-day communication in architecture.

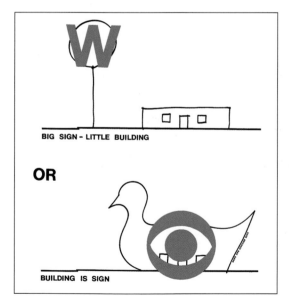

BIG SIGN - LITTLE BUILDING

OR

BUILDING IS SIGN

301. Using the Duck and Decorated Shed to study the communicative aspects of architecture has proven fruitful for us—even as we have stressed the need, while designing, to study the interplay of many other functions as well.

302. The Sainsbury Wing façade of the National Gallery can be seen, on some levels, as a billboard whose messages concern civic welcome and twentieth-century ways of relating to historical urbanism and architecture.

TASK 15: SKYLINE ELEVATION

FEBRUARY 26, 1995
WHITEHALL FERRY TERMINAL
VENTURI, SCOTT BROWN AND ASSOCIATES, ARCHITECT
ANDERSON/SCHWARTZ, ASSOCIATED ARCHITECT
NEW YORK CITY ECONOMIC DEVELOPMENT CORPORATION
vtt\task15\s-o8.dwg

0 30' 60' 120' 240'

303. The moving façade, never built, of our Whitehall Ferry Terminal, was based on LED signs. From Staten Island it would have looked like a small, bright postage stamp at the foot of the Manhattan skyline.

304, 305, 306, 307. Recent developments in the technology of LED have gone far beyond where we started in Las Vegas. We are amazed at what has been achieved on and near Times Square.

Functional relationships in the design process

Two logics of functionality—one of the immediate users, the other of the broader community—must be satisfied in any design. Resolving the issues that arise where they meet is much of the fun. Chapter 6 showed a process for defining functional relationships by understanding the patterns of activity around the site and relating them to the activities to be housed in the buildings. In that chapter, functional planning is illustrated in general terms for several projects. Here I go into greater detail for one, the Hôtel du Département de la Haut Garonne, Toulouse.

308, 309. The Hôtel du Département de la Haute-Garonne is an administrative center for a provincial government. The American equivalent would be a state capitol. The functional requirements were largely for administrative space and agency offices, where citizens and organizations could conduct their business with regional government. Then there was the legislative Salle de L'Assemblée and some unusual public uses such as a child care center. Beneath the complex was parking. There was need for formal space outdoors as well as in, and for entry places for the public arriving by foot or car. The site, within an old commercial and residential area and adjoining a new commercial node to the south, had access from the Avenue Serres, an old urban arterial; from a bridge, the Pont des Minimes over the Canal du Midi; and from smaller perimeter roads.

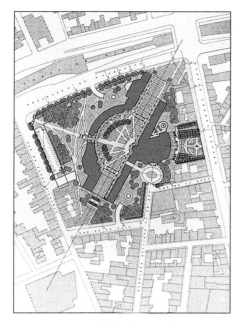

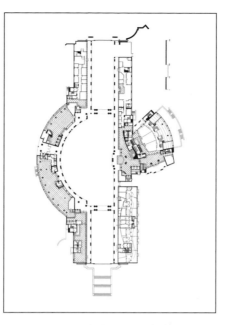

310, 311. Our first decisions were around urban functional relationships. We placed a pedestrian way diagonally across the site, linking the bridge over the canal to the area of renewal to the south. Along this way we placed the two wings of the complex. This allowed both ends of the buildings to be accessible to pedestrians from local streets. A park was on the canal side. Access points from the perimeter of the site led to the deputies' entrance and the underground parking. The child care center on the ground floor was accessible to a protected garden.

312, 313. The street through the site widened at midpoint to form a crescent-shaped plaza, giving public entry to the Salle de L'Assemblée on one side and the departmental offices on the other. There is place for sitting at its center and dark, cool shade under colonnades at its edges.

The Redefinition of Functionalism | 171

The street was both a ceremonial place and a shortcut. We hoped people would use it as part of the pathway system of the city. I hoped too that, in the Toulouse tradition, our public way would acquire an open-air market.

As I had hoped, the public and particularly schoolchildren take short-cuts via our diagonal. Sadly, market stalls were not permitted in the civic space, although they hold civic functions there. A market did occur, however, inside the building—an informal market in fruit and produce takes place in the parking structure, along the routes where people pass to the elevator. So the building generated what we had wanted, and in a logical spot, even if not quite where we had hoped.

To my surprise, shortly after the building opened, I saw our assembly hall on television in Geneva. It was the setting of a press conference announcing the introduction of a new Airbus construction project in Toulouse. Although designed as a legislative chamber, its form had generated an extra function.

Issues in defining functions and functionalism

We have seen that the definition of functionalism has wide ramifications and can be extended in many directions; that functional change is pushed by change in the social, technological, and urban dimensions of our world; and that these, in turn, exert demands on buildings to accommodate changing activities over time.

Cogent issues of definition remain: function in architecture is defined by whom, for whom, and when? Who decides what is functional or which functions to fulfill? These ultimately political questions suggest that social and community concerns and values be taken into account when building programs and functions are discussed—especially as we move from the face-to-face client to unknown "users" represented by statistics and by institutional or agency clients.

This brings up questions of scale and aggregation: who decides about function, at which scales? Society exercises controls on building in various ways and at different scales, from the region to the room. Whose

314, 315. Within the buildings most of the spaces were administrative offices. Links between the two wings were made via multistory glassed corridors, *passarelles,* that crossed the pedestrian street at either end of the central space and linked with the central corridors of the wings. At the links we placed coffee corners.

316, 317. At the center of the wing containing the assembly hall was a multistory Hall d'honneur, which lit the building lobby, tied corridors together, and served as a focal space for office workers in both wings.

318. The assembly hall was the center of a complex of spaces, serving the public, the deputies, and the President of the Département. A processional route led from the deputies' entry, to the Salle des Pas Perdus and the Salle de L'Assemblée. Below was a deputies' restaurant and a space where the building's 1,500 occupants could assemble to be addressed by the President.

obligations on us shall apply at which level, where, and when? And who has the right to decide on function for the future?

Architects have rich thoughts on function and functionalism derived from their experiences, but I have not seen these codified. I have attempted my own codification.

The complexity of the concept of function in architecture results in a lack of clarity in the definition. And I have made things worse! But the debate on functionalism and how to define it should be more broadly based and more sophisticated than it is now in architecture.

— 8 —
Context in Context

Walking in Amsterdam along a street of nineteenth-century townhouses, I noticed a single house of twentieth-century origin. Its date was hard to tell. Its lack of ornament and the proportions of its windows suggested the 1930s, but it could as easily have been a 1950s or even a 1960s version of Modernism. Then I saw that the fanlight over the front door was copied from the building next to it. This signaled a 1980s Postmodern provenance. You can tell a PoMo building because it borrows from the building next door. A Modern architect would have scorned to do this.

Postmodernism initiated a renewed discussion of context in architecture, one that concerned itself largely with borrowing from historical architecture and with fitting in to an existing context. I aim here to broaden the discussion, to give context a wider context.

I count myself lucky that, as I started architecture school, I spent time in wilderness areas where I could see no sign of human beings. Looking at the solitude of nature, I felt any building, no matter how great, would be an intrusion. Here, it seemed we human beings should nestle into the landscape, become part of it, and leave no trace. This was a nineteenth-century romantic vision to be sure, but the ecological movement has revived the concept and demanded we pay it heed. In any case, for me, consideration of context should include a no-build datum.

Context in the modern movement
Although the term was not heard in architecture before the 1970s, the early Modern movement had its own debate with context; it just did not use the word. I was taught in the late 1940s that I would have to decide whether to design buildings that stand out from the landscape, like Le Corbusier, or enter into it, like Frank Lloyd Wright. Context for my teachers was the landscape. It was seen as something the building acted upon, by either standing out or nestling in, but not as an

element in its own right having an ongoing and changing dialog with the building.

The dictionary agrees. It defines con-text, as "around a text or discourse." The center is the text. The definition suggests that what surrounds the center is inert.

This view of context as passive background was transferred by Modern architects to urbanism. The early Moderns recommended clearing the existing city and replacing it with parkland, from which their glass towers could rise unencumbered. Later, landscape became "townscape," and Modern buildings were expected to achieve a unity with the existing city despite being in contrast with it. The addition to the Gothenburg Law Courts by the architect Gunnar Asplund was of interest to architects of this mind because it adhered to the dimensions and maintained the façade plane of the existing building, yet was starkly Modern, a frame building that stood out uncompromisingly from the masonry walls beside it.

A second strain in Modernism produced prescriptions for "good manners in architecture."[1] Manners required that materials, proportions, cornice heights, wall-to-window ratios, and other regulating lines of the buildings next door be maintained in the façades of the new building, but that they be translated into a Modern idiom politely analogous to the historical surroundings. Although my generation of students called this attitude "ghastly good taste," it was widely held in Europe in the early 1950s (and remains the preferred approach to building on many U.S. university campuses in the early 2000s).

During the post–World War II rebuilding of European cities, the weight of tradition was a strong force to contend with. Reactions to it spanned from complete restoration of what had been bombed to a total turning aside into contrasting forms, with various attempts to accommodate in between. In America the need to tie into the existing city was less fiercely felt than in Europe, and for the most part U.S. urban renewal in the 1950s followed Le Corbusier's paradigm of the gleaming towers, though they were more usually surrounded by city streets or parking lots than the parks of the Ville Radieuse. Reaction to this type of urban renewal played a part in the rising concern with context among American architects and urbanists in the 1970s.

An interactive model

Robert Venturi wrote about context in 1950. He learned from Jean Labatut at Princeton in the 1940s that harmony could be achieved in architecture through contrast as well as analogy, and he developed a taste for a blend of standing out yet melding in what he later called the "gray tie with red polka dots."[2]

Bob came to believe that focusing squarely on context could enrich the design of buildings—that context had "meaning," and that each increment of new building could reinterpret and add further meaning to its surroundings. He quoted Frank Lloyd Wright, "The house did something remarkable to that site. The site was stimulating before the house went up—but like developer poured over a negative, when you view the environment framed by the Architecture of the house from within, somehow, like magic—charm appears in the landscape and will be there wherever you look. The site seems to come alive."[3]

"See context as alive and help it to be alive" seems appropriate advice to designers in the urban landscape. There are a million ways to do it. In aesthetic terms, interactions with context may be as literal as borrowing from the building next door; yet allusions can also be as fleeting as the flash of fish in water. They will probably be there whether we are conscious of them or not, but paying creative and knowing attention to context can make a richer, more relevant architecture. Over-attention, however, can produce an obsequious blandness. The architect who cares not at all for context is a boor; the one who cares only for context is a bore.

A broader context

There is more to context than physical fit. At Penn in the 1960s, social scientists and planners included the vibrant although suffering *social* city around us in the definition of urban context. At the same time, Pop Art was giving new meaning to the immediate objects of our daily lives, often by changing their contexts.

Under these influences, our "Learning from" studies took a more muscular view of context than had the Moderns. Our analyses started with the Las Vegas Strip, which we saw as the archetype of the commercial strips and auto rows to be found at the outskirts of every American city.[4] As architects studying our craft, we analyzed the physical aspects of signs and buildings on the Strip, but our view was broader than the visual, and included the economic, cultural, symbolic, and historical context. Our "Learning from Levittown" study that followed stressed the social and cultural dimensions of housing and examined how these affected its imagery and symbolism.[5]

A changing context with a life of its own

Our studies depicted contexts much larger than the buildings they surrounded. These had a vital life of their own, arising from forces that caused them to form and reform continuously—forces that would act on the individual project as well. Even if the word "context" meant no more than being with or around something, there was needed, nonetheless, an active engagement between object and context. The designer of a building or complex had the opportunity of entering into the changing context, using and adapting its meanings in the individual project and, in so doing, changing the context once again. And both would go on changing forever. An examination of fluctuating context might deliver principles and guidelines for design, to be learned from—but polka-dot fashion, not followed slavishly.

In the city, shifting patterns of activities play out as changes in both buildings and their contexts, over time. Each may change at a different rate, and this may bring about jumps in urban scale. Consider the small-town church whose tower dominates the landscape. A hundred years later it is surrounded by skyscrapers. In the process of urban change, large new buildings replace the village. This causes discontinuities that may be unsettling; yet vital cities change—background becomes foreground, history gives way to the present. The Renaissance and Baroque architecture we admire did not, for the most part, arise from green fields; medieval buildings were removed to erect them. In the tug between change and permanence there are surely few easy answers, but understanding the processes of urban change and the shifting relations between the ever-changing project and its ever-changing contexts may help.

Cultural context, cultural relevance

From the cultural context, architects can learn ways of doing things at a point in time. The conventions of building—how walls, roofs, and openings are made—can be discovered from the minor architecture of the everyday city around us. These conventions, we believe, should be followed for most building, because they are practical and culturally relevant. And, because in our time and place they derive from Modern architecture, we should, in general and in the major portions of our buildings follow Modern conventions.

On the basis of cultural relevance, we question PoMo architects' tendency to borrow indiscriminately from what is "next door," either literally or metaphorically—that is, from ideas that are intellectually or aesthetically proximate. For example, some early PoMo borrowings were from Ledoux, a French eighteenth-century architect venerated by Modernists in the 1950s, probably because his architecture looked like that of the Brutalists. But is Ledoux's work relevant to the symbolic or functional requirements of residential architecture in the United States? To us, Palladio seems a more culturally appropriate source, given the history of architectural influence between Italy and England and later between England and America. Our analyses of the sources of American housing images and symbols placed Palladio at the center in both Levittown and the Hamptons. Similarly, why did the new office buildings of the 1980s in Chicago borrow themes from Sullivan's theater there? Wouldn't the nineteenth- and early twentieth-century office buildings of the Chicago School have made a more relevant and more practical model?

Deft allusions

This is a separate argument from the one on borrowing at all and on whether and how it should be done. Although we feel borrowing—allusion—in some form or other is almost inevitable and often desirable, we criticize the heavy-handed literalness of PoMo borrowing and have looked for something lighter, and more compromised, for ourselves. For example, our extension to the London National Gallery *does* borrow from the building next door, because it is adding to it. But despite its allusion and inflection to its historical context, the Sainsbury Wing is a modern building inside and out. It uses modern structural methods and follows modern conventions in the majority of its details and spaces. Its circulation patterns and the subdivision of its spaces in plan are in important ways different from those of the historical museum it extends. Its allusions are responses to both its context and its contents—Early Renaissance paintings—and they make modern use of traditional themes. For example, the syncopated rhythms and juxtapositions of columns and openings on the façade have no equivalent in traditional architecture.

As latter-day Modernists (not Post- or Neo-), we have included communication and allusion as part of the functioning of buildings, but we try to ensure that our allusions are representations, not copies, of historical precedent, that they don't deceive. You know what the real building consists of beneath the skin or peeking out from behind the façade. Behind and around the decoration, the shed is always present, the deceit is only skin-deep and sometimes the "skin" is a surface of light without depth.

Broadening the concept

In proposing that we consider the idea of context in its context, I've suggested that the concept may be inadequate to our tasks as architects and urbanists. In its strict definition it's too object-oriented, too static. Therefore I've tried to augment the definition to maintain the value of the concept. That, in turn, has associated context with the idea of "patterns and systems" as described in Chapters 5 and 6. The broader mandate of putting context in context, then, is to work within the fluctuations of the economic, cultural, and social life around us, to understand its systems and respect the patterns they form.

We feel all buildings, even "background" buildings, should add to their context, although the appropriateness of what they add might be subject to discussion. And although some architecture stands too proud, each building should make its context better than it found it. Contextual architecture, then, becomes architecture that holds its own aesthetically and functionally within the natural and human environment, and contributes over time to its changing, pulsating patterns.

— 9 —
Essays in Context

Here follow illustrations of some attempts to engage with contexts of different types. In Perelman Quadrangle, two important elements of context were the historic buildings at the campus core and the changing patterns of activities within and around them. But there was also the five-hundred-year-old artistic context of the Houston Hall interiors. In the Toulouse Hôtel du Département, we were enchanted by the multilayered vitality of the neighborhood and by its setting against the engineering infrastructure of the bridge and canal. We were intrigued, as well, by the red brick city of Toulouse, and we learned the conventions of building there from buildings in the historic center and in the neighborhood.

At the University of Michigan, the contexts for the Palmer Drive complex were changing intellectual and activity patterns, inherited ways of building large academic structures on campus, and the multilevel topography that lay between the main campus and the medical center. In Nikko Kirifuri, the forest landscape, Japanese village streets and markets, traditional fabrics, and the paraphernalia of urban communications were sources and causes for our response.

Sometimes fitting in, sometimes standing out, we endeavored, through our designs, to leave the broader environment better, in some way, than we had found it—yet to recognize that context and building would continue to fluctuate together in a future that was unpredictable and beyond our control.

HISTORIC AND ARTISTIC CONTEXT

The Perelman Quadrangle Student Center, University of Pennsylvania, 1988–200

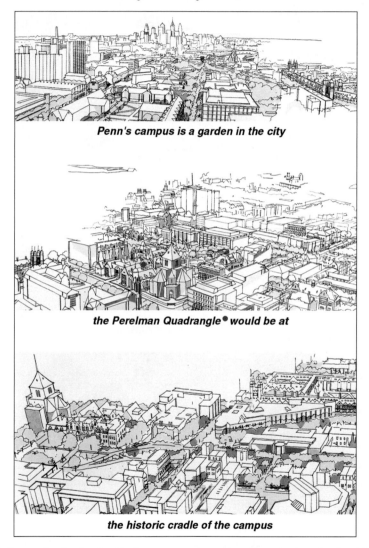

Penn's campus is a garden in the city

the Perelman Quadrangle® would be at

the historic cradle of the campus

319. Our masterplanning for the Penn campus showed how its context, regional and local within the City of Philadelphia. But it showed how activity patterns around the historic center had changed, removing Houston Hall, the student union, from pedestrian circulation ways, draining it of vitality, and reducing its plaza to an underused backwater. The Perelman Quadrangle created a student center precinct within Houston Hall and buildings around it.

320, 321. The historical photographs show how much the physical context of Houston Hall had changed over the years, but our studies suggested that strategic alterations to activity patterns and circulation systems could allow the historic center to become the hub of campus activity once again. To meet the demands of a larger, more diverse student body, we broadened the activities of the original student union and extended them into neighboring buildings.

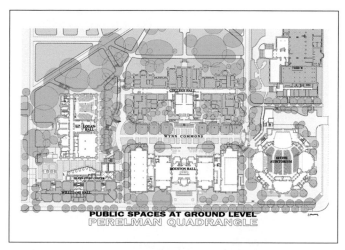

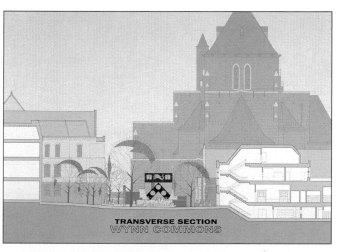

322, 323. At the center was the original Houston Hall. We pressed into student center use ground floor spaces in buildings that opened onto Houston Plaza. Together these formed Perelman Quad, a student center precinct surrounding Houston Hall. With very little new building, a center more than twice the size of the original student union was achieved.

324, 325. Houston Plaza, renamed Wynn Commons, redirected circulation ways and made the dispersed activities of the precinct read as one. We redesigned the Commons to give it a stronger, more formal identity and augmented its activities by providing chairs, steps, and low walls for sitting. At one end we placed a rostrum and at the other an amphitheater.

326, 327. From a coffee shop in Houston Hall people bring food to an outdoor terrace and to seats in the Commons beyond. You can eat a sandwich on the steps of the rostrum or amphitheater, but if someone plays a violin or gives a speech there, these become a stage and an arena.

328. Iconography for the new center included a Penn shield that formed a backdrop for the rostrum and an inscription that defined the amphitheater seating. At the entries to Wynn Commons, markers gave the history of the area and showed plans of the buildings. Other new elements were paving, trees, and lighting. Apart from these, almost everything in Perelman Quad was refurbished, not new.

329, 330. The Silfen Study Center, which includes a new study hall, café, and student activity offices, was added to Williams Hall, a 1960s classroom building at the edge of the Quad. With its glass walls, framed in iconographic blue and red metal, the Silfen Center was designed to stand out from its context and to represent something sharp and new near the historic center. Its large windows lit a major pedestrian way through a dark inner courtyard.

331, 332. Inside Houston Hall, the first two floors were restored to their original grandeur. In the basement, a new eatery was added whose kitchen and service areas extended under Wynn Commons. The existing stone walls and steel columns of the basement created an informal atmosphere different from that of the historic spaces above.

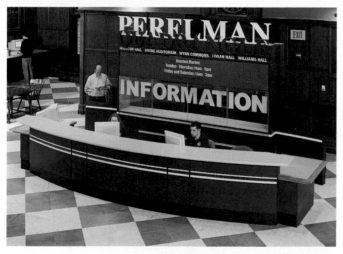

333, 334. On the ground floor, study halls made use of the inherited architecture of paneling and fireplaces to create warmth and comfort. The entry lobby extended the exterior public space of Wynn Commons into the building, making a busy concourse that formed the heart of the Perelman Quad. Here a checkerboard floor was restored and carried across the study halls, as it had been when I first saw the building—except now, at the President's request, it was in gray and white marble instead of the traditional linoleum. At least this meant it would no longer risk being replaced every ten years with biscuit-colored asphalt tiles.

335, 336. Because some people felt checkerboard patterns belonged in kitchens, we showed our client early Dutch and Flemish paintings of interiors with Jacobean linen-fold paneling and casement windows, like those on which Houston Hall was modeled. In the paintings, checkerboard tile floors led the eye to other rooms, as we hoped they would in Houston Hall. These paintings were part of the cultural context of the hall.

As we worked, a strange thing happened. While analyzing the paintings to make the argument for doing something similar, we began to see more in them than we had when we had no art-making connection with them. We discovered techniques the artist had used five hundred years earlier to direct the eye—the checkerboard floor pattern but also the shiny brass lamps overhead, light falling on people and objects from windows to one side, and the bright glowing colors of clothes and furnishings.

These influenced us as we placed a new information desk at the center of the lobby. Although it was indoors, the desk was scaled to the whole precinct and designed to be seen over the heads of people at its counter. It was to be upbeat and informative, and also to stand in contrast to the historic architecture of its direct context, the lobby.

337, 338. As its design evolved, the blue shawl and yellow skirt of the lady in Vermeer's *A Young Woman Standing at a Virginal* was reflected in our choice of colors for the shiny plastic of the desk, and the glass and moving LED lettering of the information board seemed to take the place of the sparkling chandeliers in other paintings.

339. A similar task awaited us in altering Irvine auditorium, one of the buildings of the new precinct. To adapt the hall acoustically to present-day functions, we reduced its volume, taking away seats at the side where sight lines and acoustics were problematic. The reshaping did not interfere with the famous organ or the chromatic stencil patterns, which were carefully restored. Then new elements were added: acoustical hangings from the tower, a sound-reflecting board over the stage, and others to the sides. These were multicolored too, but we used a blue and gray palette to stand out from the ochres and reds of the original stencils. The result is the richness of the polka-dot approach to context.

340. Removing the seating had produced two modest but high-ceilinged spaces on the ground floor, cut off from either side of the auditorium. These volumes we linked to the ambulatory corridor around the building to provide a coffee shop and a small recital hall. On the walls of each near the ceiling, the original auditorium stencils are visible, following the rake of the removed seating. They look like friezes on the diagonal, and they end with a high door that once gave on to the balcony. Frieze and door are mute testimony to the way the building was.

341. The basic arrangement of buildings for the Hôtel du Département derived from our analysis of the urban patterns of its context—the canal, the bridge, the avenue, the small perimeter streets, and the commercial development to the south. The decision to organize the building around a diagonal across the site was more contextual than we realized. We discovered late in the design process that there had originally been a road where we were placing our pedestrian diagonal, although it had been cleared long before we saw the site.

342. A second contextual challenge was to insert a large, civic building containing the offices of regional government into a delicate, modest part of the city—not the historic center but near it—a vital, disorderly place full of cars and alleys, modest private buildings, and enchanting vistas. Our decision to make two parallel buildings, keep their heights low, and maintain their bulk within the interior of the site was related to the scale of the environment.

343, 344, 345, 346. The result is intriguing peeks at the building from the surrounding small streets and alleys and broader vistas from the canal where the mass of the building is set against the heavy urban infrastructure of the embankment and a foreground of trees.

349, 350. The main pedestrian approach to the complex is at the point where the Pont de Minimes joins the Avenue Serres. Columns that historically marked this gateway were demolished during a street widening.

347, 348. The building contains many scales representing governmental relationships, from national to local.

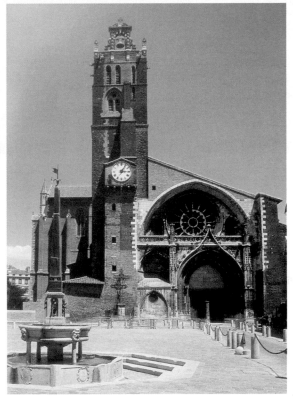

351, 352, 353, 354. In Toulouse, even the Gothic architecture is of red brick. It is a city of strong, dark shadow and bright sunlight with an amazing blue sky. (And the food! the clothes! But where was I?).

355, 356. At the outskirts, in the immediate context of our site, stucco and limestone intertwined with brick, and the overall impression was not as red as at the center of the city. Therefore for our building we mingled brick and limestone. We made the walls of the internal walkway and those at the entrance to the complex more red than the side walls, which, being visible from surrounding streets, were mainly of limestone—although they contained some red.

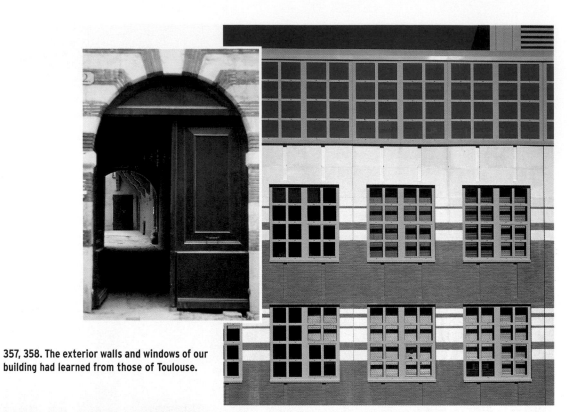

357, 358. The exterior walls and windows of our building had learned from those of Toulouse.

359, 360. Colonnades on both sides of the central way brought strong shade to the sunlit court, as we had seen them do in historic Toulouse.

361, 362. Within this red brick environment, the metal and glass *passarelles* between the two wings of the complex stood out in contrast. But all day and in changing ways they reflected the red-walled court and the sky. From the court, people could be seen passing along the *passarelles*. Under the *passarelles* was a long view of buildings in the neighborhood beyond, caught in sunlight.

363. The public entrance to the Salle de l'Assemblée was via the five-story Hall d'Honneur. Its steel and glass bow front, set within the brick of the building, was Miesian or Palladian at its center to give centrality to the entry, but on either side the glass panels included reproductions of the windows in the brick walls beside them—more polka-dots.

364, 365. The Salle required blank walls on much of its interior. Nevertheless it was glazed on the outside, along with the meeting and dining rooms beneath it and its own clerestory windows above. This steel and glass façade in a Modern idiom (a tribute to Le Corbusier?) faced the Avenue Serres across a modest place, such as you would find before a small French town hall. Façade and place made a civic gesture to the avenue. Departing from the Modern, steel members "painted" arcs across the glass wall. These, if completed, would make a circle larger than the building. They were the largest-scale element in the complex. Their pattern simulated the rainbow logo of the Département, but their scale suggested assembly at a higher level, perhaps that of the nation. Among other scales were those of the individual offices, those that welcomed individuals as they enter, and those of the Département and the community, which matched the scale of the Toulouse urban infrastructure.

Inside, most of the space was administrative and required simple subdivisions and good lighting. However, the major ceremonial spaces needed something more special, and this was achieved partly by light.

366, 367. In the windowless lower portion of the Salle, an inner layer of wall and "window" was formed. Between the inner and outer walls, acoustical material and lighting were inserted. Above was a clerestory window which revealed the bright blue Mediterranean sky but which could be screened when needed. Below, on the acoustical panels, sky and clouds were painted. So real clouds above were paralleled by painted clouds below. The cultural references for the painted sky were Magritte and the painted windows of some Renaissance and Baroque churches.

INTELLECTUAL, ACTIVITY, ARCHITECTURAL AND NATURAL CONTEXTS

The campus master plan and the palmer drive life sciences complex, the
    University of Michigan, 1997–2004

Our master plan for the University of Michigan campus dealt with context at many levels. The most obvious was the urban. The campus's 3,000
acres spread in a great diagonal across the city and region.

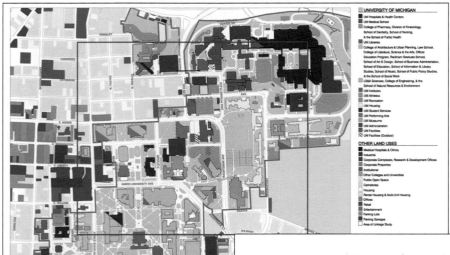

368, 369. University and city are tightly bound in a manner more common in Europe than the U.S. On one map we placed patterns of activity on campus and patterns of land uses in the city and region. Then we disaggregated and juxtaposed variables within each. For example, we overlapped a map of all housing within the city and the campus with one of retail uses in the city and dining and student facilities on campus. Transportation patterns were a second important context, particularly in areas where university growth might occur in the future.

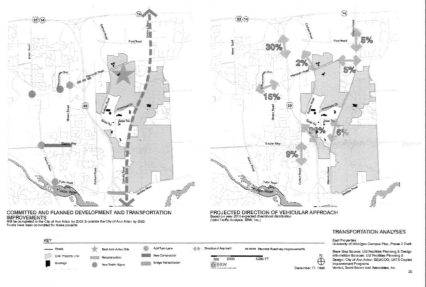

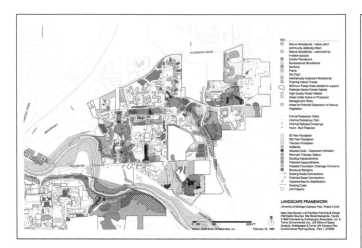

370, 371. A third was the natural environment. The original forty acres of the campus and the early grid plan of Ann Arbor sat easily on flat topography created by glaciers. But their growth patterns distorted as they reached hilly land to the east. These hills and a forty-foot drop to the Huron River flood plain below made the Medical Center campus a difficult to reach fortress and bedeviled access to the North Campus, about one and a half miles away. In addition, numerous streams and tributaries, and one wilderness fen area, required advanced thought on water management, and the university was steward as well to precious areas of forest. Overlays of these patterns gave indications of where new building was topographically feasible, where the natural heritage should be protected, and how overall patterns of campus land and water should be considered. (Our landscape and ecological consultant on this project was Andropogon. Richard Nalbandian provided specialist help, including "ground truthing.")

I have described in previous chapters how context influenced the siting and layout of the Palmer Drive Life Sciences complex and how the pedestrian ways that traverse our project knitted up and extended the macramé of the existing pedestrian circulation system, leading it from the Main campus, through our site, across the state highway, on to the Medical campus, and beyond. But I omitted one contextual variable, tuned to our own proclivities as architects. This was the architectural character of the main campus.

372. The generic, loft-like buildings of Albert Kahn, in particular, gave us special guidance in the design of the new complex, where lab buildings and classrooms predominated.

373. But we strove for only a family resemblance; our buildings were paler in color, smaller in scale (though greater in size), and they looked more modern.

374, 375. The picture of a bridge crossing a ravine to a site in a national forest shows our view of how to relate architecture to both the landscape and the cultural context. The challenge was to place this rural hotel and spa in an extremely beautiful and fragile ecology and also to respond to the Japanese cultural context near the famous temples of Nikko. Andropogon's ecological and landscape plans helped locate buildings, pathways, and roads, including the construction road, so as to leave the landscape minimally touched and able to recover from the contracting process. The bridge is modern engineering decorated by a railing that refers to the historic red bridge at the entry to Nikko.

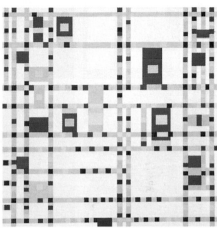

376, 377, 378. For the buildings, we looked for simplicity and modesty in line with Japanese rural architecture and the unassuming nature of the project. We felt Japanese historical buildings, those of Kyoto for example, would not be appropriate sources, because they were constructed of small wooden elements complexly pieced together and could not be reproduced economically today. To suit the relatively cheap wall-cladding materials we had to use, we evolved joint patterns that followed the structure of walls and openings of the buildings' main facades. But for the gable ends, we turned to Mondrian. Muted adaptations of several of his paintings, including *Broadway Boogie Woogie,* are visible on these wall surfaces. This was an allusion to the influences back and forth between Japan and Europe during the early years of Modernism and a salute to an enduring artistic connection. Above the patterned gables were simulated eaves and rafters, an allusion to the traditional Japanese rural pitched roofs that it did not make sense to reproduce for a slab building.

379. On the inside we learned from the markets and the everyday culture that so fascinated us in Japan.

380, 381. We treated the hotel lobby and café access area as a Japanese rural village street, designing flattened representations of the plastic or paper flowers and lanterns found on such streets. In addition we borrowed Kimono patterns from the National Museum in Tokyo, augmenting them slightly with neon to form banners, also in aluminum, that hung above the flowers. Simulations of Japanese mailboxes, public telephones, and telephone transformer boxes were added to the street to celebrate the fact that the hotel was built for the Japanese Ministry of Posts and Telecommunication. Along the street, chairs and tables were placed in rows to suggest sidewalk cafés.

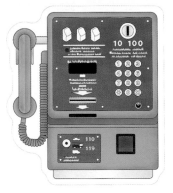

382, 383. For the guest rooms we designed carpets, floor covers, upholstery, fabrics, and wallpapers, based on Japanese rural indigo cotton fabrics.

A committee was appointed by our client to help ensure that our borrowings from the cultural context were appropriate and not ridiculous to Japanese guests. Our sources came chiefly from objects in everyday secular and ceremonial use that we had gathered or been given by friends.

384, 385. Eventually we formed an exhibition of our collection celebrating Japanese popular design.

—10 —
Mannerism, Because You Can't Follow
All the Rules of All the Systems All the Time

In this book Bob has delved into one important theme in architecture and has keyed it to a wider world. I have started broad and tried to hone to a significant center or, being me, centers. We both arrive at Mannerism. We had each come to it in our own way in our early education, and it was an interest we shared when we met. But over the span of our professional lives we have learned to see Mannerism as a theme that allows the multiple lines of our thinking to coexist and forms a framework for our theory and practice.

Bob has defined Mannerism as a series of themes; a breaking of the rules by people who know the rules well, or sometimes by naïve people who misunderstand them; a boredom with rules from knowing them so well; a disciplined breaking, limited in scope, because if all is exception, exception is not interesting; and a *need*—a necessary approach to architectural and urban design, given the complexity and contradiction of the situations in which we build.[1] He has rejected earlier notions of Mannerism as the decadent plaything of aristocrats or as an expression of neurosis.

I agree with these views and indeed collaborated in their formulation, but here I try to establish what planning disciplines might add to our evolving conception of Mannerism.[2] Coming at a definition via consideration of patterns and systems, form-function relationships, and a pulsating, supporting context, I would add that you break the rules because you can't follow all the rules of all the systems all the time, or at the same time. For one thing, some will be in conflict.

So conflict between systems is a condition that evokes Mannerism. Conflict between urban systems suggests images of clashing elements of infrastructure, of pylons, expressways, embankments, and abutments impinging on housing, shopping, and local streets. Cities have always had such juxtapositions, and they cannot be entirely domesticated. Understanding them, working to help them benefit the city, is a challenge that the early Modernists accepted (think of Saint'Elia) and we have inherited from them. For us, the challenge lends itself to Mannerism.

Questioning the rules

Adolescents ask, "Where is it written?" They respond to a parental assertion with, "On the other hand." My African and European education and the gadflies in my planning education taught me to ask the adolescents' questions, but then to add, "Whose rules? Who benefits?" And against the notion of rules they set the idea that "is" relates to "ought." They introduced the concept of passionate doubt that activates and doesn't destroy. Bob's *Complexity and Contradiction* passionately questioned received wisdom and ended with a view of living with ambiguity, and his lists of Mannerist examples, piled one on the other, purvey the same mix of passion and skepticism.

Establishing the rules

Yet to question the rules you must know them. And which rules? (Again, a planner's question.) Our response to the apparent chaos of Las Vegas was to search for underlying rules, for order *within* it. Another search could be for conventions: what are the conventions of building in Japan, or in an era of Modern architecture? How should we as architects relate to these conventions?

Rules for building and design that have lasted some thousands of years and continue to influence world architecture today are the Greek and Roman orders. My mother drew them in her architecture studio in 1928. Students did again in the 1980s. These inspired guidelines, with their rich options for extension and variation, were rediscovered by the historians of the Renaissance. Eventually Mannerist trapeze artists, having become past masters of the orders, turned the rules on their heads, perhaps in search of a new vigor, perhaps just for fun.

Breaking the rules

If expert Renaissance architects evolved Mannerism because they were bored with the rules, did a similar ennui draw some early twentieth-century architects away from the low-energy finale of the "Battle of the Styles"? The early Modern functionalists named the imperatives of industry as cause for breaking Victorian aesthetic rules, but their revolt was perhaps, as well, a search for the excitement of the uncomfortable.

So too their descendants, the Brutalists, questioned architecture's received rules and turned eventually to Mannerism.[3] The early Brutalists, and I with them, liked designs that abrogated architecture's compositional dos and don'ts—that ignored strictures against dualities, for example, or questioned whether there was only one "human scale." We enjoyed the contradictions in form, the broken rhythms, jumps in scale, and inflected, fractionated building parts that resulted from the clashing of complex urban systems. I still do.

All this, as other architects of the 1950s, tiring too of functional austerity, headed toward a flowery exaggeration of the themes of structure and function, and produced the latter-day Modernism that we criticized in *Learning from Las Vegas*.

Mount Olympus after the party

The aged industrial lands at the outskirts of great cities are not sized to us. Their scale is not "human." Elevated roads and rails; unused, polluted waterways; the remains of reed and marshland; ungainly piles of waste and vacant, disrupted buildings—these seem subject to the unruly caprice of larger-than-human users. They are playgrounds of the gods. This is the gods' Saturday night out.

Where urban systems collide, space seems residual and undefinable. Strange slivers of land are left for people and buildings. Living there is like living on a battlefield.

What do you do about following rules in these wild landscapes? They are among the most interesting and evocative of places, particularly for artists, and for architects, like Rem Koolhaas, who enjoy flying a trapeze across Olympus.

What do you do conceptually in the broader city, where so many systems, natural, physical, and social, intersect? Each has its rules. Where they clash, the city bends, sways, and totters. I am, in general, quite critical of Deconstructivism in architecture. I think it is, most of the time, mannered, not mannerist, and lacks a philosophy of finding order within chaos. It merely breaks the rules for aesthetic reasons and flounders into dullness as it does so. But I think it is at its best where urban systems bump and jar, and Decon tries to find, at the intersection, a place for human beings, even if that place doesn't look much like any we have seen before. I like Decon (or at least, the idea of it) when it's having a pillow fight with the gods.

These metaphors, and the situation of the architect in them, remind me of Emile Verhaeren's poem, "The Ship."[4] His image is of a sailor in a wild ocean:

> who, holding the helm against the wind,
> Felt the whole ship vibrate between his hands.
> He tossed on terror, death and abysses,
> In accordance with every star and every will,
> And mastering in this way the combined forces,
> Seemed to overcome and subjugate eternity.

Delusions of grandeur and drowning at sea
Planners develop sophisticated philosophies about powerlessness, but architects try to master the waves, with "master plans." Urban political actors, such as Robert Moses and Edmund Bacon, develop intrigues that powerfully push the limits, for good or ill. As urbanists and planners, we believe in orchestration, in accepting that you can't follow all the rules all the time and that there are limits to what can be controlled in the city. But as architects, we have sometimes gone down in the waves of political

action and reaction, especially in large old cities such as New York and Philadelphia.

The architect must know her or his role on a particular project in a particular city and must understand that whoever pays will be the actual client and will set the limits of the architect's power—not nice, maybe, but true. Then there are other roles. One is polemicist. This was often played by Le Corbusier, and we play it too. The limits on what we may write or show in this role are few, but there is a question as to what or whom we can influence. Between these extremes and at a variety of scales—architecture, campus planning, urban design, urban and regional planning—various roles exist. Each has its own avenues for action. If we sound, on the one side, like philosophical urban planners and, on the other, like disgruntled architects, it's true there's a certain schizophrenia between the two positions.

The clashing intersections of interests around urban "honey pot" projects is not a manageable problem. Can we make it a creative one? Only sometimes. Can one find or produce larger or smaller pools of clarity in the heaving ocean? Can one small sailor-architect make sense of the whole through an effort of mind, or will it be only a delusion of grandeur? Probably the latter. But in teams we have puzzled through the ontogeny of the Strip and, with the participation of its inner-city community, helped save Philadelphia's South Street from an expressway.[5]

To achieve more than pyrrhic victories, architects must learn what can be controlled, and how, creatively, to let go of some of what they can't control and to share the power. That's where Mannerism may help. By understanding well both the rules and the roles, the sailor may occasionally turn surfer, ride the waves as they break, find within the polity a driving force, perhaps temporary and fragile, that will let things be done along the lines of what's logical (my planner alter ego asks, "Whose logic?") despite the thousands around to help—good luck, Daniel and Nina Libeskind.

Breaking the rules well

A new approach to Mannerism in our era might start with an injunction: break the rules for good reason only. Functionalism is not dead. It's still our mantra for confronting the tasks of architecture. Unlike sculptors, we have a requirement to house people and their patterns. Yet the many-layered reality, multiplicity, and changeability of the contexts, patterns, and systems we face as architects and urbanists give us no possibility of observing all the rules all the time—not because we are arrogant but because, in our complex and contradictory world, many of the rules are in conflict. But when it comes to rule breaking, we should do it well. So there is needed a new calculus—intelligent, wise, witty, artistic, and democratic—on the justifiable breaking of the rules and how it may be done.

Meanwhile, accept that there will be areas of nonfit in a plan or design, like mistakes in a Persian rug—signs of human frailty within human grandeur. Accept that there will be what Lou Kahn called "bad spaces," now on an urban scale, and see what good and great can be plucked from them. Understand what is politically possible in your time and where you are located as architect and/or planner. Practice letting go, but carefully. Know where and when to apply this dangerous and scary philosophy. And know how to search for order within chaos and eventually, as a good Mannerist, not to quite find it.

Signs and Systems for a Mannerist Architecture for Today

Robert Venturi

In the end, here is an argument based on loves rather than ideology. Here is an argument that ultimately acknowledges an architectural aesthetic deriving from iconographic/ornamental surface rather than from dramatic/articulated form—and an aesthetic at the same time accommodating the complexity and contradiction characteristic of today via the tradition of architectural mannerism that acknowledges inconsistency within convention and ambiguity that is valid.

In the end, we're not ashamed to design buildings that look like buildings—that are:

- Naughty rather than nutty
- Mannerist rather than expressionist
- Good rather than original
- Conventional rather than heroic
- Generic rather than specific
- Iconographic rather than abstract
- Symbolic rather than formal
- Iconic rather than metallic
- Digital rather than glowing
- Informative rather than industrial
- Electronic rather than electric
- Sheltering rather than spatial
- Vivid rather than sculptural
- Responsible rather than Romantic
- Artistic rather than fashionable
- With dynamic pixels rather than decorative rivets
- Dissonant rather than *dramatique*

386. Loves

387. Rants.

- Vital rather than dramatic
- Background rather than theatrical
- Pragmatic rather than ideological
- Meaningful rather than expressionist

Denise Scott Brown

- Multi-scaled rather than "human"-scaled
- Accommodating rather than constricting
- Revelatory rather than reductive

for buildings that:

- Accommodate multiple options over generations rather than meet functional mandates for the first generation only
- Face hard problems, rather than ignore them to fit into a desired form
- Enter into a discernable and ongoing discussion with context
- Allow many interpretations rather than one truth
- Reveal rather than demonstrate.

Confronted with Bob's impassioned and copiously documented plea for signs in architecture, and with my additions of layer upon layer onto what should be thought of in design, architects will ask, "What should we *do* about all this?" We offer few answers. When I taught urban design at UCLA, our studio took a daytrip on the freeways of Los Angeles. At the end my students asked, "What are people doing about Los Angeles?" I found this puzzling. Which people? They were certainly living their lives, going about their business, planning the city—then I realized they meant, "Where is that attic where five young architects are converting Los Angeles into a linear city or some other preferred form?"

I had asked a parallel question myself. At the end of my first semester in planning school, when I realized that behind the statistics and the learned discussion on economics and politics was the fact that those in the United States who could afford houses gave little heed to the needs of those who could not, I asked, "What are you going to *do* about it?" And Professor William Wheaton, doyen of housers, walker of Washington corridors of power, drafter of legislation, replied, "I don't know. What are *you* going to do?"

Can you get *any* answers from this book? Yes, about some ways of thinking about design and about understanding patterns and working out relationships. No, about design aesthetics. Students who are grateful, at the beginning of their careers, to have simple information about planning relationships would like equivalent help with design vocabularies—the kind that comes from the magazines. But you won't find that here. Overall, our essays should show that designing is a multi-layered thing, to be learned slowly, layer by layer; but that designers must combine all the layers at once, and understand their interaction. The skilled designer keeps all the balls in the air for as long as possible in order to bring about the best resolution—if resolution is still an appropriate word after all we've said.

No, about value judgments. Another question will be, "Are the situations you've described good? Is this the way things ought to be?" In using the terms "is" and "ought" I've suggested that "ought" should derive subtly from "is," from the situation around you. I've also stressed that the "oughts" are difficult to arrive at, should not be prescribed from above, and should be allowed to well up in the process. Describing with passion (and some love) the "is"—the patterns and forces at play, the roles available, the politics—is my way of setting the stage for the judgments that designers must eventually make, in their specific roles on specific projects. It's difficult for outsiders to help individuals make value judgments. I've tried to suggest that architects be aware when they are making such judgments and use creativity in the process—but maintain understanding and humility regarding other peoples' values and their responsibility to those values. You do your best, and you augment your ideas with your education.

If an economy is a complex *social* arrangement, so is an architectural practice. Ours can be thought of as including our consultants, our hydra-headed client groups and their financial sponsors, hydra-headed construction groups, the thousands of designers in the city, and, for good or ill, the design review boards—all this in addition to the lively and creative people in our office and ourselves. Understanding one's role and options in this social organization is useful. Riding the waves and knowing how they work can help. In riding the waves, we've done different things: walked out (for good reasons but not necessarily over aesthetics); stayed in and weathered the storm; had wonderful adventures with our clients that led to great buildings (this is most of the time); been fired (it was seldom put that way); and been polemicists and pamphleteers for a cause, sometimes social and moral, sometimes aesthetic.

In our democracy there is the sincere belief that, despite the untidiness, something better will result from the ups and downs of the democratic process, including in architecture and urbanism. This is true to a point, and accepting democratic disorder has been a fruitful line of thought for us in both design and research; but, for me, that point will never include what happened to Washington, D.C., at Western Plaza or to Philadelphia at the Kimmell Center. Nevertheless, I would say *nil desperandum*. Bob might say despair all the time—but it would be the same thing.

I didn't fully cover the "rest of the ninety percent" that I defined as the subject of my chapters. The technics of architecture and the traditional arts of composition are what we spend most of our time on at the drawing board (though today it's over the printout). These include making the plan work and ensuring that the "shed" part of the building is elegant, "second-glance" architecture. We could each write a treatise on scale, another on rhythm, more on change over time in architecture, and more on the relation of public and private. Even space, about which we have proclaimed to have little interest, we could have discussed from our own point of view. I could have dealt more with social concern in architecture, but I have done that elsewhere,[1] and although I have stressed societal determinants of form here, in our architecture and planning you will find much work on architecture's environmental and technological requirements and contexts.

A PROPOSED AMERICAN SIGN MUSEUM FOR LAS VEGAS
VENTURI, SCOTT BROWN AND ASSOCIATES, INC.

388, 389. This way of illustrating our work is fairly usual, but it doesn't reveal the dimensions I have tried to describe here.

The thought in these essays applies primarily to the early schematic stages of design and planning, as the multiple layers of meaning in one's head and the repertoire of all one has seen, read, heard, thought, and dreamed gets applied to a particular problem. This thinking is needed throughout but, as the project proceeds into design development and documentation, other areas of law and expertise apply. I enjoy the development and the detailing of designs, but I find I must follow my projects to their end for the sake, as well, of the initial ideas, watching for places where the situations, the patterns, the connections I have intended are threatened. They can be lost where the needs of fire safety, for example, conflict with the desire for open and convivial eddy-points in the "street" as it runs through the building.

I am addicted to the teasing out and bringing together of all this in architecture and urbanism—challenged by the creativity required in the tasks of both analysis and synthesis. This is, finally, a commitment to the effort of will, social and individual, needed to produce beauty, a beauty that, for all the reasons I've given, is still perhaps better not admitted. Or perhaps it can now be admitted but should not be prejudiced. Design is an adventurous journey that should be allowed to have a surprising end point: arriving perhaps at a wild, unexpected beauty; or an agonized one, as when the situations are dire and imagination draws hard truth from difficult reality. This serious beauty may lie in what you see and can't, at first, accept.

It will lie, too, in the community that can be engendered, the options made available and the conversations enabled, perhaps a hundred years from now, by the connections we've not closed off, the potential we've managed to create.

— NOTES —

Introduction

1 Douglas Kelbaugh, "The Urban Context: Attention Getting," letter to the editor, *New York Times*, August 12, 2001, section 2, p. 4.

2 Marcel Proust, *La Prisonnière (The Captive)*, vol. 5 of *À la Recherche du temps perdu (Remembrance of Things Past)* (Paris: Robert Proust and Jacques Rivière, 1923), trans. C. K. Scott Moncrieff, 1929.

3 T. S. Eliot, *The Four Quartets* (London: Faber and Faber, 1944), p. 43.

4 "Learning from Las Vegas," a research studio conducted at Yale University, fall 1968, published as *Learning from Las Vegas*, by Robert Venturi, Denise Scott Brown, and Steven Izenour (Cambridge: MIT Press, 1972); rev. ed., *Learning from Las Vegas: The Forgotten Symbolism of Architectural Form* (Cambridge: MIT Press, 1977).

5 *Learning from Las Vegas*, 1977, pp. xv–xvii, and Denise Scott Brown, "Room at the Top? Sexism and the Star System in Architecture," *Architecture: A Place for Women*, ed. Ellen Perry Berkeley and Matilda McQuaid (Washington: Smithsonian Institution Press, 1989), pp. 237–246.

1. An Evolution of Ideas

1 Robert Venturi, *Complexity and Contradiction in Architecture* (New York: Museum of Modern Art and Graham Foundation, 1966).

2 Robert Venturi, Denise Scott Brown, and Steven Izenour, *Learning from Las Vegas* (Cambridge: MIT Press, 1972, 1977).

3 Robert Venturi, *Iconography and Electronics upon a Generic Architecture: A View from the Drafting Room* (Cambridge: MIT Press, 1996).

4 I am grateful to Martin Filler for his understanding review of the book in *The New York Review of Books*, October 23, 1997.

2. Communication and Convention for an Iconographic Architecture

1 Le Corbusier, *Towards a New Architecture* (1923; trans. Frederick Etchells, 1927; London: Architectural Press, 1946), p. 37.

2 Ibid.

3 Henry Russell Hitchcock, Jr., *The Architecture of H. H. Richardson and His Times* (New York: The Museum of Modern Art, 1936), p. 303.

4 Marilyn Aronberg Lavin, *The Place of Narrative: Mural Decoration in Italian Churches, 431–1600* (Chicago: The University of Chicago Press, 1990).

5 Hitchcock, *The Architecture of H. H. Richardson and His Times*, p. 301.

6 Vincent Scully, *Modern Architecture and Other Essays*, ed. Neil Levine (Princeton: Princeton University Press, 2003), p. 29.

7 Hitchcock, *The Architecture of H. H. Richardson and His Times*, p. 302.

8 Ibid., p. 301.

9 Douglas Kelbaugh, "Psycho-Architecture: Public Needs First," letter to the editor, *New York Times*, December 5, 1999, section 2, p. 4.

10 Douglas Kelbaugh, "The Urban Context: Attention Getting." letter to the editor, *New York Times*, August 12, 2001, section 2, p. 4.

11 Douglas Kelbaugh, postscript to original draft, ibid., July 29, 2001, not published.

12 Vincent Scully, "Robert Venturi's Gentle Architecture," *The Architecture of Robert Venturi*, ed. Christopher Mead (Albuquerque: University of New Mexico Press, 1989), p. 15.

13 Ralph Waldo Emerson, "The American Scholar," oration delivered before the Phi Beta Kappa Society in Cambridge, Massachusetts, August 31, 1837, in *Essays and English Traits*, ed. Charles W. Eliot, Harvard Classics, vol. 5 (New York: Collier, 1909), p. 21.

4. A New Mannerism, for Architecture as Sign

1 Robert Venturi, *Complexity and Contradiction in Architecture* (New York: Museum of Modern Art and Graham Foundation, 1966), p. 19.

2 Alan Plattus and Alan Chimacoff, "Learning from Venturi," *Architectural Record*, September 1983, pp. 88–97.

3 Nicholas Pevsner, *An Outline of European Architecture* (London: Penguin Books, 1990), p. 209.

4 Arnold Hauser, *Mannerism, the Crisis of the Renaissance and the Origin of Modern Art* (Cambrige: Harvard University Press, 1986), p. 18.

5 William Mitchell, "Fair dinkum Aussie," *RIBA Journal* 110: 18.

6 Vincent Scully, "Robert Venturi's Gentle Architecture," *The Architecture of Robert Venturi*, ed. Christopher Mead (Albuquerque: University of New Mexico Press, 1989), p. 26.

5. Some Ideas and Their History

1 In the 1972 introduction to *Learning from Las Vegas*, we aligned ourselves unequivocally with early Modernism, even as we criticized its later directions. By 1978 Bob

had firmly claimed to talk "as a Modern architect, not a Postmodern or neo-Beaux-Arts architect," cf. "Learning the Right Lessons from the Beaux Arts," *Architectural Design*, January 1979, pp. 23–31; talk given at the Architectural Association, London, 1978. By "Modern," we mean the Modern Movement in architecture and its altered but appropriate forms for today. We use "modern" to mean up-to-date.

2 Dan Jacobson, "Introduction," in Olive Schreiner, *The Story of an African Farm* (1883; London: Penguin, 1971), p. 18. It may once have been part of the American experience. The African questions, "How can we find our own idiom?" and "How should we relate to the arts of Europe and America?" may have been important in America 150 years ago, although in architecture they seem to have force here still today.

3 South Africans in those days would have said "European." The American term "Western," which figures in the debate on multiculturalism, refers to the cultures of Western Europe and Northern America, not to the American West.

4 The Festival of Britain, 1951, was a celebration of the end of the war and an attempt to bolster the nation's achievements in the arts, science, and industry.

5 *Family and Kinship in East London* (London: Routledge and Kegan Paul, 1957).

6 Alison Smithson, ed., "Team 10 Primer," *Architectural Design*, December 1962, rpt. in *Team 10 Primer* (Cambridge: MIT Press, 1968). Denise Scott Brown, "Team 10, Perspecta 10, and the Present State of Architectural Theory," *Journal of the American Institute of Planners*, January 1967, pp. 42–50. Denise Scott Brown, "Learning from Brutalism," *The Independent Group: Postwar Britain and the Aesthetics of Plenty*, ed. David Robbins (Cambridge: MIT Press, 1990), pp. 203–206 (see all articles in this book). Sarah Williams Goldhagen and Réjean Legault, eds., *Anxious Modernisms: Experimentation in Postwar Architectural Culture* (Montreal and Cambridge: Canadian Centre for Architecture and MIT Press, 2000).

7 CIAM *(Congrès International d'Architecture Moderne)* was founded in 1928 by the early Modernists to propagate their ideas on architecture and urbanism.

8 I have described it in "Lavorando per Giuseppe Vaccaro," *Edilizia Popolare* 243 (January/February 1996): 5–13; and in "Imparare da Vaccaro," in *Giuseppe Vaccaro*, ed. Marco Mulazzani (Milan: Electa, 2002), pp. 66–75.

9 Where and when did Kahn first come across Brutalist and Team 10 thought? History puts it in September 1959 at the last CIAM conference in Otterloo. But from my experience at Penn and from examining sequential designs of the Richards Laboratory, I suspect that something of Brutalism reached him in some way two or three years before that.

10 Everything changed in June 1959, when Robert Scott Brown was killed. South Africa and the world lost a true-hearted patriot and the potential of a brilliant architect and planner.

11 The 1960s was the decade of social change in the United States. Its early start at Penn owes in part to Philadelphia's Liberal Democratic Reform government of the 1940s, to the New Deal experience of some of the Planning Department's elder statespeople, and to the Chicago University planning training of some of its younger members. There is a good story to be told of a "Philadelphia School" of architecture and urbanism that is broader than the one described in the architectural press.

12 Denise Scott Brown, "The Meaningful City," *Journal of the American Institute of Architects*, January 1965, pp. 27–32.

13 Bob's Theories of Architecture course, given 1961–1966, was perhaps the first theory course in any American school of architecture. From it—from the closing section of each lecture, where the young architect said what *he* stood for—grew *Complexity and Contradiction in Architecture*.

14 I have described Penn's planning and urban design studios and various others I have devised in "Between Three Stools: A Personal View of Urban Design Practice and Pedagogy," in *Education for Urban Design* (Purchase, NY: Institute for Urban Design, 1982), pp. 132–172. This was republished, with other related essays, in *Urban Concepts: Denise Scott Brown*, an *Architectural Design* Profile, *Architectural Design* 60:1–2:90. London: Academy Editions, 1990.

7. The Redefinition of Functionalism

1 Although, as we have said, there is a strong admixture of both of us in both parts of this book, the idea of the generic palazzo, dome, and basilica and what we can learn from them belong particularly to Robert Venturi. See Chapter 4.

2 Robert K. Merton, "Manifest and Latent Functions," in *Social Theory and Social Structure* (Glencoe, IL: Free Press, 1949).

3 Personal communication with Karin Theunissen, Delft University of Technology, and http://www2.holland.com/us/index.html?page = http://www2.holland.com/us/arts/modern/vannelle.html.

4 Bob liked the alliteration of the two names, but he uses Gropius as a generic early Modernist. Gropius certainly did write in this vein, although I heard exasperated exclamations from Jane Drew, his one-time partner, when I lectured on this subject in 1977, and it's true that a later Gropius reinstated "delight" as a component rather than a resultant—he went soft, as the early Brutalists would have said.

5 Kevin Lynch, "Environmental Adaptability," *AIP Journal* 24:1 (1958).

6 See Robert Venturi, Chapter 1, on the subject of the generic urban grid and the Philadelphia grid in particular.

8. Context in Context

1 A. T. Edwards, *Good and Bad Manners in Architecture* (London: J. Tiranti Ltd., 1944), was a source for this approach, although Edwards himself was not a Modernist.

2 Robert Venturi, "Context in Architectural Composition," master's thesis, Princeton University, 1950. See as well Chapter 1 above.

3 I have not found the source of this quotation.

4 "Learning from Las Vegas," a research studio conducted at Yale University, fall 1968, published as *Learning from Las Vegas* (Cambridge: MIT Press, 1972).

5 Yale University, spring 1970; it was published as "Remedial Housing for Architects' Studio," *Venturi, Scott Brown and Associates: On Houses and Housing* (London: Academy Editions, 1992; New York: St. Martin's Press, 1992), pp. 51–57.

10. Mannerism, Because You Can't Follow All the Rules of All the Systems All the Time

1 In Chapters 1 and 4 above.

2 Why the capital M? We use Mannerism to denote a Late Renaissance style and now also a definable, latter-day architectural philosophy, in spirit with historical Mannerism. By contrast, mannerism could be an attitude to politics or social life. Bob differentiates between explicit Mannerism and implicit mannerism in Chapter 4. Comparable differences would be between Classical and classical, Modern and modern.

3 See Chapter 5, above.

4 My rough translation of

> qui maintenait à contre-vent la barre,
> Sentait vibrer tout le navire entre ses mains.
> Il tanguait sur l'effroi, la mort et les abîmes,
> D'accord avec chaque astre et chaque volonté,
> Et, maîtrisant ainsi les forces unanimes,
> Semblait dompter et s'asservir l'éternité.

The Oxford Book of French Verse, ed. St. John Lucas (London: Oxford University Press, 1907; rev. 1957), pp. 516–517.

5 The sad story has yet to be told of how community participation changed, from poor people in inner cities trying to save their houses to upper-middle class professionals, with their lawyers, trying to maintain their property values and the aesthetic status quo. It's many years since I have heard "the poor" mentioned at community meetings.

Conclusion

1 Issues of social concern were seamed throughout our studies of Las Vegas, though some readers have found them hard to recognize there. The same is true, and I hope will be more obvious, in this book. Here is a brief selection from perhaps two dozen articles, written 1963–2003, where I have explicated my approach to social questions in architecture and urbanism: "Natal Plans," *Journal of the American Institute of Planners*, May 1964, pp. 161–166 (on planning in South Africa); "An Alternate Proposal that Builds on the Character and Population of South Street," *Architectural Forum*, October 1971, pp. 42–44; "On Architectural Formalism and Social Concern: A Discourse for Social Planners and Radical Chic Architects," *Oppositions 5*, Summer 1976, pp. 99–112; "From Memphis, Down the Mississippi to the World," *Memphis: 1948–1958* (Memphis: Brooks Museum of Art, 1986), pp. viii–xi; "The Public Realm, the Public Sector and the Public Interest in Urban Design" in *Urban Concepts: Denise Scott Brown*, An *Architectural Design* Profile, *Architectural Design* 60:1–2:90 (London: Academy Editions, 1990); "The Rise and Fall of Community Architecture," in *Urban Concepts*, ibid.; "Honor the Mother," *APA Planning*, December 1995, pp. 4–5; "The Power of Inner Diversity," *AIArchitect*, May 1996, p. 22 (opening address, 1995 Diversity Conference); "Philadelphia's Battle against Blight: Define the Issue and Focus on Maintenance," *Philadelphia Inquirer*, May 7, 2000.

— BIBLIOGRAPHY —

This is a listing of some books and articles that are mentioned in the text, or are sources for ideas discussed here, or have been meaningful to us over the years. The Venturi, Scott Brown and Associates website, www.vsba.com, illustrates projects, thought, and writing of the firm. A bibliography of writings about the firm and its work, as well as writings by members of VSBA, dating from the 1950s to the present, can be found at www.vsba.com/whoweare/index_biblio.html.

Banham, Reyner. *Theory and Design in the First Machine Age*. Cambridge: MIT Press, 1960.

Burnham, Daniel Hudson, and Edward H. Bennett. *Plan of Chicago*, ed. Charles Moore. Chicago: Commercial Club, 1909.

Crane, David A. "Chandigarh Reconsidered: The Dynamic City." *Journal of the American Institute of Planners*, November 1960, pp. 280–292.

———"The City Symbolic." *Journal of the American Institute of Planners*, May 1960, pp. 32–39.

Davidoff, Paul. "Advocacy and Pluralism in Planning." *Journal of the American Institute of Planners*, November 1965, pp. 331–338.

———and Thomas Reiner. "A Choice Theory of Planning." *American Institute of Planners Journal*, May 1962, pp. 103–115.

Egbert, Donald Drew. *Social Radicalism and the Arts: Western Europe—A Cultural Revolution from the French Revolution to 1968*. New York: Alfred A. Knopf, 1970.

Eliot, T. S. *The Four Quartets*. London: Faber and Faber, 1944, p. 43.

Emerson, Ralph Waldo. "The American Scholar," an oration delivered before the Phi Beta Kappa Society at Cambridge, Massachusetts, August 31, 1837. In Charles W. Eliot, ed., *Essays and English Traits*, Harvard Classics, vol. 5. New York: Collier, 1909, p. 21.

Gans, Herbert J. *The Levittowners: Ways of Life and Politics in a New Suburban Community*. New York: Columbia University Press, 1967.

———*People and Plans: Essays on Urban Problems and Solutions*. New York: Basic Books, 1968.

———*Popular Culture and High Culture: An Analysis and Evaluation of Taste*. New York: Basic Books, 1974.

———*The Urban Villagers: Group and Class in the Life of Italian-Americans*. New York: The Free Press of Glencoe, 1962.

Goodman, Paul, and Percival Goodman. *Communitas: Means of Livelihood and Ways of Life*. New York: Vintage Books, 1947, rev. 1960.

Hauser, Arnold. *Mannerism: The Crisis of the Renaissance and the Origin of Modern Art.* Cambridge: Harvard University Press, 1986.

Hitchcock, Henry Russell, Jr. *The Architecture of H. H. Richardson and His Times.* New York: The Museum of Modern Art, 1936.

Isard, Walter. *Location and Space Economy: A General Theory Relating to Industrial Location, Market Areas, Land-Use, Trade, and Urban Structure.* Cambridge: MIT Press, 1956.

Jackson, John Brinckerhoff. *Discovering the Vernacular Landscape.* New Haven: Yale University Press, 1984.

———*The Interpretation of Ordinary Landscapes: Geographical Essays,* ed. D. W. Meinig. New York: Oxford University Press, 1979.

———*Landscapes: Selected Writings of J. B. Jackson,* ed. Ervin H. Zube. Amherst: University of Massachusetts Press, 1970.

———*The Necessity for Ruins and Other Topics.* Amherst: University of Massachusetts Press, 1980.

Koolhaas, Rem. "Lagos (Harvard Design School Project on the City)," in Rem Koolhaas, Stefano Doeri, Sanford Kwinter, Nadia Tazi, and Daniela Fabricius, *Mutations.* Barcelona: Actar Editorial, 2001, pp. 650–720.

———Chuihua Judy Chung, Jeffrey Inaba, and Sze Tsung Leong, eds.. *The Harvard Design School Guide to Shopping.* Cologne: Taschen, 2001.

Korn, Arthur. *History Builds the Town.* London: Lund, Humphries, 1953.

Kouwenhoven, John A. *The Beer Can by the Highway.* New York: Doubleday, 1961.

Kriesis, Paul. *Three Essays on Town Planning.* St. Louis: Washington University School of Architecture, May 1963.

Lavin, Marilyn Aronberg. *The Place of Narrative: Mural Decoration in Italian Churches, 431–1600.* Chicago: University of Chicago Press, 1990.

Le Corbusier. *Towards a New Architecture,* 1923, trans. Frederick Etchells, 1927. London: Architectural Press, 1946.

Lilla, Mark. "The Great Museum Muddle." *New Republic,* April 8, 1985, pp. 25—30.

Lynch, Kevin. "Environmental Adaptability." *AIP Journal* 24, no. 1 (1958).

MacLean, Alex. *Designs on the Land: Exploring America from the Air.* New York: Thames and Hudson Press, March 2003.

———and Bill McKibben. *Look at the Land: Aerial Reflections on America.* New York: Rizzoli International Publications, 1993.

Mitchell, R. B., and C. Rapkin. *Urban Traffic: A Function of Land Use.* New York: Columbia University Press, 1954.

Moore, Charles W. "You Have to Pay for the Public Life." *Perspecta* 9/10 (1965): 57–106.

Mumford, Lewis. *Roots of Contemporary American Architecture.* New York: Grove Press, 1959.

Myerson, Martin, and Edward C. Banfield. *Politics, Planning and the Public Interest: The Case of Public Housing in Chicago.* Glencoe, IL: Free Press, 1955.

Pevsner, Nicholas. *An Outline of European Architecture.* London: Penguin Books, 1943.

Robbins, David, ed. *The Independent Group: Postwar Britain and the Aesthetics of Plenty.* Cambridge and London: MIT Press, 1990.

Scott Brown, Denise. "Architectural Taste in a Pluralistic Society." *Harvard Architectural Review*, Spring 1980, pp. 41–51.

————"Learning from Pop," and "Reply to Frampton." *Casabella*, May–June 1971, pp. 14–46. Rpt. in *Journal of Popular Culture*, Fall 1973, pp. 387–401, and in Robert Venturi and Denise Scott Brown, *View from the Campidoglio*. New York: Harper and Row, 1984, pp. 26–34.

————"On Architectural Formalism and Social Concern: A Discourse for Social Planners and Radical Chic Architects." *Opposition 5* (Summer 1976): 99–112.

————"Team 10, Perspecta 10, and the Present State of Architectural Theory." *Journal of the American Institute of Planners*, January 1967, pp. 42–50.

————*Urban Concepts: Denise Scott Brown*, an *Architectural Design* Profile, *Architectural Design*, 60:1–2:90. London: Academy Editions, 1990.

Scully, Vincent. *Modern Architecture and Other Essays*, ed. Neil Levine. Princeton: Princeton University Press, 2003.

————*The Shingle Style: Architectural Theory and Design from Richardson to the Origins of Wright.* New Haven: Yale University Press, 1955.

Seeger, Charles. "Toward a Unitary Field Theory for Musicology." *Selected Reports*, Institute of Ethnomusicology, 1, no. 3 (1970): 171–210.

————"Tractatus Esthetico-semioticus," *Current Thought in Musicology*, ed. J. W. Grubbs and L. Perkins. Austin: University of Texas Press, 1976.

Smithson, Alison, ed. "Team 10 Primer," *Architectural Design*, May 1960, pp. 175–205. Rpt. in *Team 10 Primer*. Cambridge: MIT Press, 1968.

————and Peter Smithson. *Uppercase 3*. London: Whitefriar Press, 1960.

Summerson, John. *Georgian London*, 3rd ed. Cambridge: MIT Press, 1978.

Tufte, Edward R. *The Visual Display of Quantitative Information.* Chesire, CT: Graphics Press, 1983.

————*Visual Explanations: Images and Quantities, Evidence and Narrative.* Chesire, CT: Graphics Press, 1997.

Tyrwhitt, Jacqueline, ed. *Patrick Geddes in India* (extracts from official reports on Indian cities, 1915–1919). London: Lund, Humphris, 1947.

Venturi, Robert. *Complexity and Contradiction in Architecture.* New York: Museum of Modern Art and Graham Foundation, 1966.

————*Iconography and Electronics upon a Generic Architecture: A View from the Drafting Room.* Cambridge: MIT Press, 1996.

————Denise Scott Brown, and Steven Izenour. *Learning from Las Vegas.* Cambridge: MIT Press, 1972; rev. 1977. (1972 edition contains description of South Street project.)

Wagner, Philip L. *The Human Use of the Earth.* Glencoe, IL: The Free Press, 1960.

Webber, Melvin M. "Comprehensive Planning and Social Responsibility." *American Institute of Planners Journal* 29, no. 4 (1963): 232–241.

————"The New Urban Planning in America." *Town Planning Institute Journal* 54 (January 1968): 3–10.

Wilson, Chris, and Paul Groth, eds. *Everyday America: Cultural Landscape Studies after J. B. Jackson.* Berkeley: University of California Press, 2003.

Wolfe, Tom. *The Kandy-Kolored Tangerine-Flake Streamline Baby.* New York: Farrar, Straus and Giroux, 1965.

Young, Michael, and Peter Willmott. *Family and Kinship in East London.* London: Routledge and Kegan Paul, 1957.

— ILLUSTRATION CREDITS —

Thank you to all the photographers, authors, and photography stock companies that provided the artwork for this book. A note about credit for artwork: this has been given for hand-drawings. Yet, because architecture is a collaborative process, crediting "the hand" in a drawing has always been problematic, particularly for complex projects that take years to design and build. And the advent of computer-generated artwork has only made the process of assigning credit more difficult. Though the art may be created on a computer rather than a drafting board, the necessary graphic and aesthetic decision-making process remains the same. Whatever the medium, Robert Venturi and Denise Scott Brown are largely responsible for the "VSBA style" of presentation drawings. Denise Scott Brown directs the design and content of VSBA's planning graphics, maps, and mapped information.

1. The Historical Society of Pennsylvania (HSP). Thomas Holme's "Plan of Philadelphia" [Of610. 1683]
2. Thomas Cole (American, born England, 1801–1848). *The Architect's Dream*, 1840, oil on canvas, 53x84$\frac{1}{16}$ in. Toledo Museum of Art. Purchased with funds from the Florence Scott Libbey Bequest in Memory of her Father, Maurice A. Scott. 1949.162
3. Thomas Cole (American, born England, 1801–1848). *The Architect's Dream*, 1840, oil on canvas, 53x84$\frac{1}{16}$ in. Toledo Museum of Art. Purchased with funds from the Florence Scott Libbey Bequest in Memory of her Father, Maurice A. Scott. 1949.162. Augmented by VSBA
4. Anthony Scibilia / Art Resource, NY
5. Erich Lessing / Art Resource, NY. *Composition with Red, Blue, and Yellow*, 1930, oil on canvas, 46x46 cm. Kunsthaus Zurich / © Mondrian / Holtzman Trust c/o hcr@hcrinternational.com
6. © 2004 Artists Rights Society (ARS), New York / ADAGP, Paris / FLC
7. Hans Hildebrandt
8. Unknown
9. © 2004 Artists Rights Society (ARS), New York / ADAGP, Paris / FLC
10. © 2004 Frank Lloyd Wright Foundation, Scottsdale, AZ / Artists Rights Society (ARS), NY
11. Derek Croucher / CORBIS
12. Christian Richters Fotograf

13. Eduard Hueber
14. © 1993. Cindy Lewis
15. VSBA
16. VSBA
17. VSBA
18. VSBA
19. VSBA
20. Drawing by Robert Venturi / VSBA
21. Drawing by Robert Venturi / VSBA
22. Richard Cummins / Corbis
23. VSBA
24. Erich Lessing / Art Resource, NY
25. Matt Wargo / VSBA
26. Scala / Art Resource, NY
27. Sandro Vannini / Corbis
28. Erich Lessing / Art Resource, NY
29. Giraudon / Art Resource, NY; Art Resource, NY
30. Marilyn Aronberg Lavin. *The Place of Narrative: Mural Decoration in Italian Churches, 431–1600.* Chicago: University of Chicago Press, 1990
31. Scala / Art Resource, NY
32. Unknown
33. Giraudon / Art Resource, NY
34. Country Life Picture Library
35. Adam Woolfitt / Corbis
36. Catherine Karnow / Corbis
37. Jack E. Boucher / Historic American Buildings Survey, Library of Congress
38. Unknown
39. VSBA
40. VSBA
41. VSBA
42. Bettmann / Corbis
43. Bettmann / Corbis
44. Scala / Art Resource, NY
45. Matt Wargo / VSBA
46. Matt Wargo / VSBA
47. Matt Wargo / VSBA
48. Drawing by Denise Scott Brown / VSBA
49. Drawing by Robert Venturi / VSBA
50. Scala / Art Resource, NY
51. Scala / Art Resource, NY
52. The Andy Warhol Foundation, Inc. / Art Resource, NY
53. Julie Marquart / VSBA
54. © 2004 Artists Rights Society (ARS), New York / ADAGP, Paris / FLC
55. © 2004 Artists Rights Society (ARS), New York / ADAGP, Paris / FLC
56. Rollin La France
57. Jack E. Boucher / Historic American Buildings Survey, Library of Congress
58. Drawing by Robert Venturi / VSBA
59. Drawing by Robert Venturi / VSBA
60. Lawrence S. Williams / VSBA
61. Matt Wargo / VSBA
62. William Watkins / VSBA
63. Drawing by Gerod Clarke and Arthur Jones / VSBA
64. VSBA
65. VSBA
66. VSBA
67. Drawing by W. G. Clark and Robert Venturi / VSBA
68. VSBA
69. VSBA
70. VSBA
71. Tom Bernard / VSBA
72. Tom Bernard / VSBA
73. Tom Bernard / VSBA
74. Drawing by Robert Venturi / VSBA
75. John Dargis
76. VSBA
77. Christian Richters Fotograf
78. Tom Bernard / VSBA
79. Tom Bernard / VSBA
80. Unknown

81. Tom Bernard / VSBA
82. Tom Bernard / VSBA
83. Drawing by Frederic Schwartz and Robert Venturi / VSBA
84. Matt Wargo / VSBA
85. Matt Wargo / VSBA
86. Matt Wargo / VSBA
87. VSBA
88. VSBA
89. VSBA
90. Matt Wargo / VSBA
91. Matt Wargo / VSBA
92. Matt Wargo / VSBA
93. Unknown
94. Drawing by John Chase / VSBA
95. Matt Wargo / VSBA
96. Matt Wargo / VSBA
97. VSBA
98. VSBA
99. Koji Horiuchi
100. PhotoKosuge
101. Koji Horiuchi
102. VSBA
103. Matt Wargo / VSBA
104. VSBA
105. VSBA
106. Matt Wargo / VSBA
107. Matt Wargo / VSBA
108. Matt Wargo / VSBA
109. Matt Wargo / VSBA
110. David Graham
111. David Graham
112. VSBA
113. VSBA
114. VSBA
115. VSBA
116. Drawing by Robert Venturi / VSBA
117. Drawing by Robert Venturi / VSBA
118. Drawing by Robert Venturi / VSBA
119. VSBA
120. VSBA
121. VSBA

122. Martin Hürlimann / © 2004 Artists Rights Society (ARS), New York / ProLitteriz Zurich
123. Angelo Hornak / Corbis
124. Edwin Smith / RIBA Library Photographs Collection
125. Image Select / Art Resource, NY
126. Scala / Art Resource, NY
127. Edwin Smith / RIBA Library Photographs Collection
128. Edwin Smith / RIBA Library Photographs Collection
129. A. F. Kersting
130. Country Life Picture Library
131. Courtesy of the Trustees of Sir John Soane's Museum
132. Photoservice Electa, Milano
133. Photoservice Electa, Milano / Andrea Jemolo
134. Fondo Moretti, Archivio Centrale Dello Stato, Roma
135. Courtesy Henry Millon
136. Courtesy Carolina Vaccaro
137. Richard Weston, *Alvar Aalto* (London: Phaidon Press, 1995).
138. Richard Weston, *Alvar Aalto* (London: Phaidon Press, 1995).
139. Nicola Coldstream, *Medieval Architecture* (New York: Oxford University Press, 2002).
140. Scala / Art Resource, NY
141. Historic American Buildings Survey, Library of Congress
142. The City Archives of Philadelphia, Record Group 78: Photographic collection
143. The Historical Society of Pennsylvania (HSP)
144. Unknown
145. Scala / Art Resource, NY
146. *Michelangiolo Architetto*. Giulio Einaudi, 1964

147. *Michelangiolo Architetto.* Giulio Einaudi, 1964
148. Scala / Art Resource, NY
149. SEF / Art Resource, NY
150. Photoservice Electa, Milano
151. *Michelangiolo Architetto.* Giulio Einaudi, 1964
152. *Michelangiolo Architetto.* Giulio Einaudi, 1964
153. Photoservice Electa, Milano
154. *Michelangiolo Architetto.* Giulio Einaudi, 1964
155. Andrea Palladio. *The Four Books on Architecture*
156. Bertotti Scamozzi. *Le Fabbriche ei disegni di Andrea Palladio, Vicenza, 1776–1783*
157. Bertotti Scamozzi. *Le Fabbriche ei disegni di Andrea Palladio, Vicenza, 1776–1783*
158. Norman F. Carver, *Japanese Folkhouses*
159. Bob Krist / Corbis
160. VSBA
161. VSBA
162. VSBA
163. Ken Straiton / Corbis
164. Viviane Moos / Corbis
165. Steven Izenour / VSBA
166. Steven Izenour / VSBA
167. Ronald Evitts
168. Drawing by W. G. Clark / VSBA
169. Steven Izenour / VSBA
170. Historical Picture Archive / Corbis
171. Ronald Evitts
172. Giuseppe Bovini. *Ravenna Treasures of Light.* Ravenna: Longo, 1991
173. VSBA
174. Timothy Soar
175. Matt Wargo / VSBA
176. Timothy Soar
177. Denise Scott Brown / VSBA
178. Robert Scott Brown / VSBA
179. Denise Scott Brown / VSBA
180. Denise Scott Brown / VSBA
181. Denise Scott Brown / VSBA
182. Robert Scott Brown / VSBA
183. Philadelphia City Planning Commission
184. Chicago Area Transportation Study 1959 (CATS)
185. Chicago Area Transportation Study 1959 (CATS)
186. Courtesy Walter Isard
187. Courtesy Walter Isard
188. Chicago Area Transportation Study 1959 (CATS)
189. Robert Scott Brown / VSBA
190. Philadelphia City Planning Commission
191. Drawing by Denise Scott Brown / VSBA
192. Drawing by Denise Scott Brown / VSBA
193. VSBA
194. Courtesy Walter Isard
195. Philadelphia City Planning Commission
196. Landis Aerial Surveys
197. Louis I. Kahn Collection, The University of Pennsylvania and the Pennsylvania Historical and Museum Commission
198. VSBA
199. VSBA
200. VSBA
201. VSBA
202. VSBA
203. VSBA
204. VSBA
205. VSBA
206. VSBA
207. VSBA
208. VSBA

209. VSBA
210. Giambattista Nolli. *Map of Rome, 1748.*
211. VSBA
212. VSBA
213. Louis I. Kahn Collection, The University of Pennsylvania and the Pennsylvania Historical and Museum Commission
214. VSBA
215. Steven Izenour / VSBA
216. VSBA
217. VSBA
218. Matt Wargo / VSBA
219. VSBA
220. VSBA
221. VSBA
222. VSBA
223. VSBA
224. VSBA
225. VSBA
226. Matt Wargo and David Graham / VSBA
227. 1963. Central Campus Planning Study, University of Michigan of Johnson, Johson, and Roy / The Bentley Historical Library, University of Michigan
228. VSBA
229. Dale Fisher
230. VSBA
231. VSBA
232. VSBA
233. VSBA
234. VSBA
235. VSBA
236. VSBA
237. Frederick Olmstead papers / The Bentley Historical Library, University of Michigan
238. 1963. Central Campus Planning Study, University of Michigan of Johnson, Johnson, and Roy / The Bentley Historical Library, University of Michigan
239. VSBA
240. VSBA
241. VSBA
242. VSBA
243. VSBA
244. VSBA
245. VSBA
246. VSBA
247. VSBA
248. VSBA
249. VSBA
250. VSBA
251. VSBA
252. Daniel Brewer
253. Daniel Brewer
254. Daniel Brewer
255. Daniel Brewer
256. Daniel Brewer
257. Daniel Brewer
258. Daniel Brewer
259. Daniel Brewer
260. Daniel Brewer
261. Drawing by Robert Venturi / VSBA
262. VSBA
263. VSBA
264. VSBA
265. Drawing by Robert Venturi / VSBA
266. Kevin Fleming / Corbis
267. Giambattista Nolli. *Map of Rome, 1748*
268. VSBA
269. VSBA
270. VSBA
271. VSBA
272. VSBA
273. VSBA
274. Denise Scott Brown
275. Drawing by Denise Scott Brown / VSBA

276. Drawing by Robert Venturi / VSBA
277. VSBA
278. Rauner Special Collections, Dartmouth College Library
279. VSBA
280. Matt Wargo / VSBA
281. Based upon a diagram by GPR Laboratory Planners
282. Eisner & Gallion. *The Urban Pattern*, 1950. This material is used by permission of John Wiley & Sons, Inc.
283. VSBA
284. Louis I. Kahn Collection, The University of Pennsylvania and the Pennsylvania Historical and Museum Commission / Collection R. H. Donnelly Erdman
285. Louis I. Kahn Collection, The University of Pennsylvania and the Pennsylvania Historical and Museum Commission
286. Courtesy Carolina Vaccaro
287. Louis I. Kahn Collection, The University of Pennsylvania and the Pennsylvania Historical and Museum Commission
288. Mixed Photographers: Grand Rond Productions; Kawasumi Architectural Photography Office; Matt Wargo
289. Matt Wargo / VSBA
290. Matt Wargo / VSBA
291. Matt Wargo / VSBA
292. Drawing by Robert Venturi / VSBA
293. VSBA
294. VSBA
295. VSBA
296. VSBA
297. VSBA
298. VSBA
299. VSBA
300. VSBA
301. VSBA
302. Matt Wargo / VSBA
303. VSBA
304. Alan Schein Photography / Corbis
305. Steven Izenour / VSBA
306. Ronald Evitts
307. Steven Izenour / VSBA
308. Grand Rond Productions
309. Matt Wargo / VSBA
310. VSBA
311. VSBA
312. Matt Wargo / VSBA
313. Matt Wargo / VSBA
314. Matt Wargo / VSBA
315. Matt Wargo / VSBA
316. Matt Wargo / VSBA
317. Matt Wargo / VSBA
318. Matt Wargo / VSBA
319. VSBA
320. University of Pennsylvania Archives
321. Matt Wargo / VSBA
322. VSBA
323. VSBA
324. Matt Wargo / VSBA
325. Drawing by Don Jones and Michael Wommack / VSBA
326. Matt Wargo / VSBA
327. Julie Marquart / VSBA
328. Matt Wargo / VSBA
329. Matt Wargo / VSBA
330. Matt Wargo / VSBA
331. Matt Wargo / VSBA
332. Matt Wargo / VSBA
333. Matt Wargo / VSBA
334. Matt Wargo / VSBA
335. Pieter de Hooch, Dutch, 1629–1684. *Potrait of a Family Making Music*, 1663, oil on Canvas, 98.7x116.7cm. © The Cleveland Museum of Art, Gift of the Hanna Fund. 1951.355

336. Johannes Vermeer, 1632–1675. *A Lady at the Virginals with a Gentleman*, RCIN 405346, CW 230. WC 109. The Royal Collection © 2004 Her Majesty Queen Elizabeth II

337. Johannes Vermeer, 1632–1675. *A Young Woman standing at a Virginal.* © National Gallery, London

338. Matt Wargo / VSBA

339. Julie Marquart / VSBA

340. Julie Marquart / VSBA

341. Grand Rond Productions

342. Matt Wargo / VSBA

343. Matt Wargo / VSBA

344. Matt Wargo / VSBA

345. Matt Wargo / VSBA

346. Matt Wargo / VSBA

347. Matt Wargo / VSBA

348. Matt Wargo / VSBA

349. Unknown

350. Matt Wargo / VSBA

351. Unknown

352. Unknown

353. Unknown

354. Unknown

355. Matt Wargo / VSBA

356. Matt Wargo / VSBA

357. Matt Wargo / VSBA

358. Unknown

359. Unknown

360. Matt Wargo / VSBA

361. Matt Wargo / VSBA

362. Matt Wargo / VSBA

363. Matt Wargo / VSBA

364. Matt Wargo / VSBA

365. Matt Wargo / VSBA

366. Matt Wargo / VSBA

367. Matt Wargo / VSBA

368. VSBA

369. VSBA

370. VSBA

371. VSBA

372. VSBA

373. VSBA

374. Kawasumi Architectural Photograph Office

375. Kawasumi Architectural Photograph Office

376. Shinkenchiku-sha

377. Digital Image © The Museum of Modern Art / Licensed by SCALA / Art Resource, NY. *Broadway Boogie-Woogie*, 1942–43, oil on canvas, 127x127 cm. © Mondrian / Holtzman Trust c/o hcr@hcrinternational.com

378. PhotoKosuge.

379. VSBA

380. Shinkenchiku-sha

381. VSBA

382. VSBA

383. Kawasumi Architectural Photograph Office

384. Matt Wargo / VSBA

385. Matt Wargo / VSBA

386. VSBA

387. VSBA

388. Matt Wargo / VSBA

389. VSBA

— ACKNOWLEDGMENTS —

VSBA would like to thank and acknowledge the Architects of Record for the following illustrated projects: Anlyan Center for Medical Research, Yale University: Payette Associates, Inc.; California NanoSystems Institute, UC Santa Barbara: Altoon + Porter Architects; Children's Museum of Houston: Jackson and Ryan, Architects; Clinical Research Building, University of Pennsylvania: Payette Associates, Inc.; Gonda (Goldschmied) Neuroscience and Genetics Research Center, UCLA: Lee, Burkhart, Liu, Inc.; Hôtel du Département de la Haute-Garonne: Hermet-Blanc-Delagausie-Mommens/Atelier A4; Michigan Stadium Extension, University of Michigan: Hellmuth, Obata, Kassabaum, Sport Inc.; Mielparque Nikko Kirifuri Resort: Marunouchi Architects & Engineers, Associated Architects; New York City Office Tower Competition: Nobutaka Ashihara, Associates; Palmer Drive Life Sciences Complex, University of Michigan: Smith Group; Desman Associates (parking structure); Times Square Hotel Project: Emery Roth and Sons, Architects; U.S. Embassy for Berlin Competition: Einhorn Yaffee Prescott, A&E, P.C. Would that there were enough room in this book to list all the associated architects, consultants, and technical advisors who provided invaluable assistance over the years.

Thank you to all the students and colleagues who participated in the research studios discussed from the "Learning from Las Vegas" studio at Yale University and from the "West Philadelphia" studio at the University of Pennsylvania. And to the UC Berkeley group who devised and acted the illustrations for "Functions of a Table."

Of course there would be no projects to discuss if not for the clients who commissioned VSBA. These are the clients for the completed projects illustrated in this book: Bard College; BASCO, Inc.; Best Products Company, Inc.; Children's Museum of Houston; Citizens' Committee to Preserve and Develop the Crosstown Community; City of Columbus, IN; City of Trenton Fire Department; Weld Coxe and Mary Hayden; Département of Haute-Garônne; Friends Neighborhood Guild; Grands

Restaurant; Harvard University; Institute for Scientific Information; Japanese Ministry of Posts and Telecommunications; Knoll International; Lehigh Valley Hospital System; McDonalds Corporation; Memphis Center City Commission; National Gallery, London; New York City Economic Development Corporation; Oberlin College; Princeton University; Marion "Kippy" Stroud; University of California, Los Angeles; University of California, Santa Barbara; University of Delaware; University of Michigan; University of Pennsylvania; Vanna Venturi; Whitney Museum of American Art; Williams College; Yale University.

And thank you to the many architects, planners, interns, drafts-people, photographers, and support staff who called our offices home over the years: Hidenao Abe, Michael Ablon, David Achterberg, Jeanne Adams, Ian Adamson, Elise Adibi, Patash Ahmed, William Algie, Eli Allen, John Anderson, John Andrews, Margo Angevine, Courtney Anspach, Adam John Anuszkiewicz, Chris Appleford, Tony Atkin, Deborah Aukee, Eric Aukee, Joeri Aulman, Matthew Baker, Penny Baker, Jean Barker, Edward Barnhart, John Bastian, Faith Baum, Thomas Beck, Andrew Benner, Lynn Bensel, Tom Bernard, Catherine Murray Bird, Harry Bolick, Charles Boney, Daniel Borden, Ralitsa Boteva, Anthony Bracali, James Bradberry, Joshua Brandfonbrener, Joe Bratina, Anne Bress, Luke Brewer, David Brisbin, Jason Brody, Stephanie Brown, Steve Brown, Venita van Hamme Brown, Virginia Brown, Rick Buckley, Mark Burgess, Roc Caivano, Theo Calvin, Alexander Campagno, Laura Campbell, Sheila Campbell, Bryan Cannon, Colin Cathcart, Peony Chan, John Chase, Arthur Chen, Greg Chiselko, Linna Choi, Yoocheol Choi, Angelina Chong, Stephanie Christoff, Edward Chuchla, Gerod Clarke, Heather Clark, Matthew Clark, Terrance Clark, W.G. Clark, Peter Clement, Seth Cohen, Janet Colesbury, Rodney Collins, Giovanni Cosco, Catherine Cosentino, Brett Crawford, Claudia Cueto, Jeffrey Current, Nicole Dandridge, David Dashiell, John Dasilva, Jill Dau, John Defazio, Leslie DeLong, Mary Dempsey, Bob Desilets, Kathy Dethier, Betsy DeWitt, Dennis DeWitt, Peter DiCarlo, Justin Diles, Amy Dubble, Timon

Duffield, Elise DuPont, Meredith Elbaum, Jane Epstein, Andrew Erstad, Stephen Estock, Ronald Evits, Peter Exley, Ke Feng, Eric Fiss, Diane Fitzgerald, Gunther Flaig, John Folan, Annemarie Foley, John Forney, David Fox, Ike Foy, David Franke, Jennifer Friedman, Emily Fuller, Peter Funk, Silvia Fuster, Timur Galen, Susan Gallagher, Sean Gannon, Steve Gatschet, Erica Gees, Ion Ghika, Stephen Glascock, Judith Glass, Nancy Goldenberg, Diane Golomb, Christine Gorby, Kevin Gray, Andrea Greer, James Greifendorf, Gary Griggs, Michael Guarino, Mark Gurin, Johnathan Hancock, Arthur Hanlon, Tamika Hardy, Sam Harris, Douglas Hassebrook, Vince Hauser, Michael Haverland, Laurie Hawkinson, Jeffrey Hawver, John Hayes, Joseph Herrin, Mark Hewitt, Dante Hightower, David Hinson, Adam Hirsch, Jeffrey Hirsch, Paul Hirshorn, Elizabeth Hitchcock, Susan Hoadley, Stephanie Hodal, Jake Hokanson, Keith Hone, Monica Hoover, Daniel Horowitz, Dione Hosler, HoLynn Hsu, Agatha Hughes, Stanford Hughes, Frances Hundt, Christopher Hunt, John Hunter, Ann Izenour, Elisabeth Izenour, John Izenour, Steven Izenour, Tessa Izenour, Saul Jabbawy, Lauren Jacobi, Virginia Jacobs, Mytili Jagannathan, Thomas Jerin, Ben Johanson, Eric Johnson, Arthur Jones, Brian Jones, Don Jones, John Jones, Kimberley Jones, Thomas Jones, Richard Kase, Frank Kawasaki, Tim Kearney, Elica Keebler, Steven Kieran, Sun Joo Kim, Jim King, Jennifer Kinkead, Atsuhiro Kishimoto, Amy Klee, Gary Kneeland, Mark Kocent, Douglas Kochel, James Kolker, Benjamin Kracauer, Jeffrey Krieger, Thomas Kuhar, Kate Kulpa, Perry Kulper, Brian Labau, David Labe, Reyhan Larimer, Shirley Lauman, Cheryl Lawrence, Michael Legrand, Tse-Chiang Leng, Ryan Levasseur, Michael Levin, Eva Lew, Jeffrey Lewis, James Liebman, Tim Lisle, Alana Litwak, Susan Lockwood, Sara Loe, Jill Loman, Lynette Lopez, Corbett Lyon, Deanna Mabry, Joe Malase, Noa Maliar, David Manker, Robert Marker, David Marohn, Julie Marquart, Mayva Marshall-Moreno, Christine Matheu, Missy Maxwell, Andrew McAllister, Jeffrey McBride, Christian McClellan, Daniel McCoubrey, Ronald McCoy, Meredith McCree, Sharon McGinnis, Rosa McGrail, Louisa McIlwaine, Nataki McNeal, Gordon Meehl, Pablo Meninato,

Katrina Menkes, Adam Meyers, Tim Mock, Richard Mohler, Matthew Morong, Whitney Morrill, Catherine Moy, Alice Mueller, Paul Muller, Guy Munsch, Julie Munzner, Catherine Murdock, Brian Newswanger, Jason Nguyen, Mindy No, Amy Noble, Matthew Nowaczyk, Scott Ogburn, Carolyn Okine, Felisa Opper, Scott Osbourne, Eric Oskey, Lucy Ovens, Cynthia Padilla, Gabrielle London Palitz, Catherine Paplin, Andrew Pasonick, Lynda Payne, Fred Pearsoll, Elester Pearson, Nathalie Peeters, Anthony Pellecchia, Willis Pember, Willis Pemky, David Perkes, Michael Peters, Ricky Peterson, Anthony Pett, Layng Pew, Joan Pierpoline, Christine Pietrucha, Carol Pinard, Marc Pinard, Elizabeth Plater-Zyberk, Karen Pollock, Debbie Presser, Michael Price, John Pringle, Roger Pryor, Thomas Purdy, Robert Puzauskie, Beth Rahe, Helen Wallace Ralston, William Rankin, Daniel Rauch, John Rauch, Lee Rayburn, Frances Read, John Reddick, Christine Reed, Robert Renfro, Charles Renfro, Richard Rice, Miles Ritter, Louis Rodolico, Frances Roosevelt, David Rosenberg, George Ross, Glenda Rovello, Stan Runyan, Annette Rusin, Jeffrey Ryan, Lourdes Saladino, Ivan Saleff, Susan Scanlon, David Schaaf, Suzie Schickedanz, Mark Schimmenti, Mark Schlenker, James Schmidt, Ellen Schneider, Matthew Schottelkotte, Garreth Schuh, Robert Schultz, Frederic Schwartz, Dan Scully, Jamila Sefiane, Maria Segal, Douglas Seiler, Matthew Seltzer, Heidi Gilbert Sentivan, Gregory Shakoor, Delano Shane, Colleen Shannon, Thomas Shay, Kairos Shen, Karsang Sherpa, David Singer, Paulette Singley, Christopher Smith, Ian Smith, Makai Smith, Douglas Southworth, Tamra Spencer Larter, Nina Sprecher, Steven Stainbrook, Mark Stankard, Harris Steinberg, Elysia Steward, Richard Stokes, Alexander Stolyarik, Jean Suh, Melanie Swick, Nancy Szostek, Mat Szwajkos, Stanley Taraila, Jeremy Tenenbaum, Eric Thompson, Georgia Thorsen, John Thrower, Andrew Thurlow, Simon Tickell, James Timberlake, David Tinley, Nancy Rogo Trainer, Huyen Tran, Linh Tran, Howard Traub, Ghislaine Trombert, Ann Trowbridge, Tsung-Ming Tung, Darcelle Tyler, Jonathan Usuka, Monica Vandergrift, Stephen van Dyck, David Vaughan, Terry Vaughan, Rebecca Vieyra, Jon Wagner,

Ingalill Wahlroos, James Wallace, Matt Wargo, Keith Weibrecht, Amy Weinstein, Maurice Weintraub, Erin Wieand, Mark Wieand, Steven Wiesenthal, Jim Williamson, Sherry Williamson, James Winkler, Chris Wise, Wai-kwan Wong, Kenneth Wood, Malcolm Woollen, Tony Wrice, Brian Wurst, Jeffrey Wyant, Mirai Yasuyama, Noriyuki Yasuyama, Mary Yee, Joy Yoder, Carey Jackson Yonce, Aaron Young, Michael Yung. We have worked hard to create a complete list, but undoubtedly a few individuals have been missed. Please accept our thanks in any case, and let us know who you are and when you worked here.

— INDEX —

Italic type indicates a figure caption.

Aalto, Alvar, Vuoksenniska church , 81, *137, 138*

Africa, 105-108, 112, 113, 114, 213; Zulu kraal, 152; Mapoch tribe village, *181;* Bulawayo, representation of, *182;* Kwazulu, *189*

Alberti, Leon Battista, Palazzo Rucellai, *44*

Albini, Franco, 111

Allen Memorial Art Museum addition, 47–48, 71, *72*

Amiens Cathedral, *33*

Andropogon, *370, 375*

Anlyan Center for Medical Research and Education, 68, *112*

Architects, Designers, and Planners for Social Responsibility, 115

Architectural Association, 109

Asplund, Gunnar, Gothenburg Law Courts, 176

Bacon, Edmund, 215,

Bard College, Stevenson Library, 56, *91*

BASCO Showroom and Warehouse, 50, 70, 76

Beethoven, Ludwig van, 10, *386*

BEST Showroom, 50, *79*

Bibliothèque Ste. Geneviève, 58

Blake, Peter, 35

Blenheim Palace, 81, *130*

Borromini, Francesco, Re Magi chapel, 81, *132, 133*

Boston, West End, 113

Brandenberg Gate, 63

Brasini, Armando, Church of the Cuore Immacolato di Maria Santissima, 85, *144*

Breuer, Marcel, Whitney Museum of Art, 48

Brinkman, J., Van Nelle Factory, 150–151, 152, 162, *274*

Broadacre City, Frank Lloyd Wright, *10,* 16

Brown, Jeffrey and Elise Jaffe, viii

Browne, Stanhope, viii

Brunelleschi, Filippo, Duomo, 38, *51*

Bryn Mawr College dormitories, 117, 161, *213, 284*

Butterfield, William, 81

California NanoSystems Institute, 68, *114*

Capitoline Hill, 87, *149*

Casa del Girasole, 41, 81, *134*

Castle Ashby, *34*

Cefalù cathedral, 24, *26,* 85, *140*

Chicago, 179

Chicago Area Transportation Study, *184, 185, 188*

Children's Museum of Houston, 56, *90*

Chimacoff, Alan, 74

Christaller, Walter, *194*

Christ Church, Spitalfields, 81, *128*

Church of the Sacré Coeur, 16

Church of the Cuore Immacolato di Maria Santissima, 85, *144*

Church of the Immaculate Conception, 81, *135*

Church of the Jacobins, 85, *139*

CIAM (Congres Internationaux d'Architecture Moderne), 111

Cohen, Ziona, v

Cole, Thomas, *The Architect's Dream,* 2, 12,

College of William and Mary, Main Building, 36, *43*

Columbus, Indiana, Fire Station #4, 44, *64*

Commercial Vernacular, *14, 18,* 34

Coxe-Hayden House and Studio, 51, *81*

Crane, David, v, 113, 116, 117, 160, *209,*

Dacca, Bangladesh, 117

Davidoff, Paul, v, 118,

DeGolyer, Everett, v

Doric Temple shed, Mount Desert Island, 48, *75*

Dulwich Picture Gallery, 53

Duck and Decorated Shed, 8, *20,* 35, *41, 42,* 94, 152, *301*

Duomo, 38, *51*

Eames, Charles, 51

Eames, Ray, 51

Egbert, Donald Drew, viii

Egyptian architecture, 24, *24,* 58

Emerson, Ralph Waldo, 39

Emory Roth & Sons, 94

England, 107, 109. *See also specific works*

Erick van Egeraat associated architects (EEA), MeZZ popstage, *12*

Fagus Shoe Works, 7, 14

Farnsworth House, 41, *57*

Fascist architecture, 25

Federation Square, Melbourne, 97, 99

Finkelpearl, Philip and Kitty, v

Fire Station #4, 44, *64*

Frist Campus Center, Princeton University, 66, *108, 109, 226*

Furness, Frank: Pennsylvania Academy of the Fine Arts, 55, 85, *142*; National Bank of the Republic, 85, *143*; Furness Building, University of Pennsylvania, 117, 161-162, 164, *289, 290*

Galansky, Jane, v

Gans, Herbert, v, 113, 146

Gianopulos, Nicholas, viii

Ginza, 94

Glass, Judith, viii

Glazer, Nathan, vii

Gloucester Cathedral, 77, 78, *122*

Goldfinger, Ernö, 142

Gonda (Goldschmied) Neuroscience and Genetics Research Center, UCLA, *46, 280*

Gordon Wu Hall, Princeton University, 51, *82*

Gothenburg Law Courts, 176

Grand's Restaurant, 43, *60*

Greek temples, 24, *51*

Gropius, Walter, 145, 151, *265*; Fagus Shoe Works, 7, 14

Guarini, Guarino, Church of the Immaculate Conception, 81, *135*

Guggenheim Museum, 161

Guild House, 43, *62*

Hansen, Tomkin, and Finkelstein house, 106, *177*

Hardwick Hall, 79, *123*

Harris, Britton, viii

Harvard University: Massey Lectures, vii; Massachusetts Hall, 36; Sever Hall, 36; Loker Commons, Memorial Hall, 58–59, *95*

Hatfield House, 79

Hauser, Arnold, 74

Hawksmoor, Nicholas: Christ Church, Spitalfields, 81, *128*; St. George's Bloomsbury, 81, *129*

Hitchcock, Henry Russell, 17, 35–36

Horowitz, Barney, viii

Hôtel du Département de la Haute-Garônne, 56–58, *92*, 170-172, 182, *308–318, 341–367*

Howe, George, PSFS Building, 25, *37*

Hughes, Thomas and Agatha, viii

Independent Group, 109

Institute for Scientific Information, 50, *78*

Interstate 95, *15*, 34

Isard, Walter, viii

Isle de la Cité, 16

Izenour, John, viii

Izenour, Steven, v, *Learning from Las Vegas*, 8, 13, *20*, 34, 40, 41, 215

Izutsu, Akio, v, 61

Jackson, J. B., v, 36

Jacobi, Lauren, viii

Jacobs, Jane, 109, 113

Jacobson, Dan, 107

Jaffe, Elise and Jeffrey Brown, viii

Japan, 25, 85, 93–94, 214, *378, 381*. *See also specific works*

Johannesburg, South Africa, 105, 106, 107

Johnson, Johnson & Roy, *238*

Johnson, Philip, 52

Jones, Inigo, St. Paul's Church, 79, *124*

Kahn, Albert, *372*

Kahn, Louis I., 110, 112–113, 115–117, 147, *197*, 218, *287, 288*; Richards Medical Research Laboratories, 37, *46*, 113, *285*; Bryn Mawr College dormitories, 117, 161, *213, 284*; Salk Institute, *285*

Kelbaugh, Douglas, 38

Kellett, Morris, viii

Knoll Showroom, Knoll Furniture, 51, *80*

Kohn, Pederson & Fox: Morgan Stanley Building, 94, *164*; Morgan Stanley Dean Witter Building, 94, *165–167*

Kolker, Jamie, v

Koolhaas, Rem, 215

Korn, Arthur, v, *History Builds the Town*, 110

Krautheimer, Richard, viii

Kunsthaus Bregenz, *13*

Kyoto, Japan, 25, 93, *378*

Labatut, Jean, 7, 177

Labroust, Henri, Bibliothèque Ste. Geneviève, 58

Lakofski, Lily, v

Lakofski, Phyllis Hepker, v

Lakofski, Shim, v

Lancaster County, Pennsylvania, *193*
Las Vegas Strip: circa 1968, 8, 9, *293–298;*
    circa 1970, *16, 17, 18;* circa 2000, *22;* VSBA
    interpretation of, *23, 389;* and South Africa,
    107; and Scott Brown, 118; and context, 178;
    complexity of, *196;* and communication, *198,
    200, 299, 300;* churches in, *201, 202;* land-
    use plan of, *205, 206;* Nolli maps of, *211,
    212*
Laurentian Library, 86–87, *147, 148*
Lavin, Marilyn Aronberg, *The Place of
    Narrative,* 24, *30*
Le Corbusier, 7, 105, 110, 142, 153, 175, 176,
    216, *365;* Villa Savoye, *4, 14,* 41; *Towards a
    New Architecture, 6,* 14; Ville Radieuse, *9,*
    15–16, *54, 55*
Ledoux, Claude-Nicolas, 179
Lehigh Valley Hospital, 69, *115*
L'Enfant, Pierre Charles, 11
Lescaze, William, PSFS Building, *25, 37*
Levittown, Pennsylvania, 179
Lewis, Sydney and Frances, viii
Libeskind, Daniel, 216
Libeskind, Nina, 216
Loker Commons, Memorial Hall, Harvard
    University, 58–59, *95*
London, East End, 109, 113
Long Island Big Duck, 35, *41*
Longleat House, 79
Los Angeles, 220
Lösch, August, *194*
Low House, 41, 85, *141*
Lutyens, Sir Edwin, 77, 81
Lynch, Kevin, 153–154
Mackintosh, Charles Rennie, 81

Magritte, René, *367*
Marcus, Manfred, v
Martienssen, Rex, 105
Massachusetts Hall, Harvard University, 36
Massey Lectures, vii
McCoubrey, Daniel, v
McDonald's, 65, *107*
McKim, Mead and White, Low House, 41, 85,
    141
Memphis, Tennessee, *208*
Merton, Robert, 113, 146
Meyerson, Martin, viii
MeZZ popstage, *12*

Michelangelo, 77; Porta Pia, 8, 87, *153, 154;*
    St. Peter's, 38, *50,* 86, *145, 146;* Laurentian
    Library, 86–87, *147, 148;* Capitoline Hill, 87,
    149; Sforza Chapel, Santa Maria Maggiore,
    87, *150–152*
Mielparque Nikko Kirifuri Resort Hotel and
    Spa, 60–61, *99–101,* 182, *374–385*
Mies van der Rohe, Ludwig, 147, *285;*
    Farnsworth House, 41, *57*
Miletus, *282*
Mitchell, Robert, viii, 116
Mitchell, William, 97, 99
MoMA Queens, 50, 77
Mondrian, Piet: *Composition with Red, Blue, and
    Yellow, 5,* 14; *Broadway Boogie-Woogie,* 61, *378*
Montacute House, 79
Moretti, Luigi, Casa del Girasole, 41, 81, *134*
Morgan, Sherley, viii
Morgan Stanley Building, 94, *164*
Morgan Stanley Dean Witter Building, 94,
    165–167
Morong, Matt, viii
Moses, Robert, 215
Nalbandian, Richard, *370*
Nassau Hall, Princeton University, 36
National Bank of the Republic, 85, *143*
National Gallery, 99–100. *See also* Sainsbury
    Wing, National Gallery
Neue Sachlichkeit, 110, 111
New Brutalists, 110, 111, 112, 113, 114, 151,
    179, 214
New York City, 94, *187. See also specific works*
Nigeria, 116
Nikko, Japan, 93
Nolli, Giambattista, *210,* 267, 268
Nolli map, *211, 212, 214, 216*
Nowicki, Matthew, 162
Olmstead, Frederick Law, study of University
    of Michigan, *237*
Palazzo di Propaganda Fide, 81
Palazzo Rucellai, *44, 386*
Palazzo Valmarana, 91, *155*
Palladio, Andrea, 77, 86, 179; Palazzo
    Valmarana, 91, *155;* Il Redentore, 92, *157,
    386;* San Giorgio Maggiore, 92, *156*
Panthéon, 16
Pargiter, Dorothy, v
Pariser Platz, 63
Penn, William, *1,* 11, *197*

Pennsylvania Academy of the Fine Arts, 55, 85, *142*

Perkins, G. Holmes, viii

Pevsner, Nikolaus, 74

Philadelphia: of William Penn, *1*, 11, *197;* plan of, *1*, 152, *183*, *190;* Baltimore Pike, 11; Chester Avenue, 11; Lancaster Avenue, 11; loft factory building in, *45;* land-use in, *195;* South Street, *207*, 217; West, *277*, *283;* row houses in, *284*

Philadelphia Museum of Art, 24, *25*, 40, 46, 55

Philadelphia Orchestra Hall project, 54–55, *87*, *88*

Philadelphia World's Fair, 1976, 46

Piano, Renzo, Pompidou Center, *11*

Piazza San Marco, 96, *170*

Plattus, Alan, 74

Pompidou Center, *11*

Porta Pia, 8, 87, *153*, *154*

Poussin, Nicolas, 46

Princeton University: Nassau Hall, 36; Gordon Wu Hall, 51, *82;* Frist Campus Center, 66, *108*, *109*, 226

PSFS Building, 25, *37*

Putney, Paul, viii

Quaroni, Ludovico, 112

Rapkin, Chester, viii, *195*

Il Redentore, 92, *157*, *386*

Re Magi chapel, 81, *132*, *133*

Richards Medical Research Laboratories, University of Pennsylvania, 37, *46*, 113, *285*

Richardson, H. H.: Sever Hall, 36; Trinity Church, 44

Rogers, Richard, Pompidou Center, *11*

Romano, Giulio, 77

Rome, 24, 93, *210*, *267*

Russian Constructivists, *8*, 15, 25

Sainsbury Wing, National Gallery, 53–54, *86*, 99–100, *173–176*, 180, *214–218*, *302*

Salk Institute, *285*

La Sainte Chapelle, *29*

San Giorgio Maggiore, 92, *156*

San Gregorio Barbarigo, 81, *136*, *286*

San Vitale, *172*

Schreiner, Olive, *The Story of an African Farm*, 107–108

Scanlon, Sue, viii

Scott Brown, Denise: *Learning from Las Vegas*, 8, 13, *20*, 34, 40, 41, 215; "The Meaningful City," 116

Scott Brown, Robert, 111, 112

Scully, Vincent, viii, 35, 39, 100

Seeger, Charles, v

Sever Hall, Harvard University, 36

Sforza Chapel, Santa Maria Maggiore, 87, *150–152*

Sir John Soane House and Museum, 81, *131*

Smithson, Alison, 109

Smithson, Peter, 109, 110, 112, 118

Soane, Sir John, Dulwich Picture Gallery, 53; Sir John Soane House and Museum, 81, *131*

South Africa, 105, 112, *178–181*

Spear, Richard, 47

St. Apollinare Nuovo, *27*, *28*

St. George's Bloomsbury, 81, *129*

St. Paul's Cathedral, 79, *125*, *126*

St. Paul's Church, 79, *124*

St. Peter's, 38, *50*, 86, *145*, *146*

St. Stephen's Walbrook, 79, *127*

Stevenson Library, Bard College, 56, *91*

Team 10, 110, 111, 113, 114

Tenenbaum, Jeremy, viii

Thomas, George, viii

Thompson, Doris, v

Thousand Oaks City Hall and Civic Center, 45–46, *67*

Times Square, New York, 52, 94, 96–97, *169*, *171*, *304–307*

Tokyo, Japan, 85, 93–94

Toulouse, France, *93*, *172*

Trabant Student Center, University of Delaware, 59, *96*

Trafalgar Square, London, 53

Trainer, Nancy Rogo, v

Trenton Central Fire Headquarters and Museum, 64, *106*

Trinity Church, 44

Trubek House, 51

University of California, Berkeley, 118

University of California, Los Angeles, 152, 221; Gonda (Goldschmied) Neuroscience and Genetics Research Center, 46, *280*, *281*

University of California, Santa Barbara: California NanoSystems Institute, 68, *114*

University of Delaware, Trabant Student Center, 59, *96*

University of Michigan, 203, *227–232*, *237*, *238*, *368*, *369;* football stadium extension, 66–67, *110*, *111;* Palmer Drive Life Sciences complex, 183, 204, *233–236*, *239–251*, *370*,

371, 373; Life Sciences Institute, *241, 242, 250;* Commons Building, *250*

University of Pennsylvania, 113–116, 131, 146, 152, 177, *219–222, 224;* Richards Medical Research Laboratories, 37, *47,* 113, *285;* Clinical Research Building, 52, *84, 85;* Perelman Quadrangle, 63, *103,* 183, *225, 319–336, 338–340;* Wynn Commons, *103, 324–328, 331–334;* Furness Library, 117, 162; Fisher Fine Arts Library, 162; Furness Building, 162, 164, *289, 290;* Houston Hall, 183, *224, 319–324, 326, 327, 331, 332, 335, 336;* Williams Hall, *223, 224, 329, 330;* College Hall, *224;* Houston Plaza, *224, 322–325;* Irvine Auditorium, *224, 225, 339, 340;* Silfen Study Center, *329, 330*

Vaccaro, Giuseppe, 112; San Gregorio Barbarigo, 81, *136,* 152, *286*

Vanbrugh, Sir John, Blenheim Palace, 81, *130*

Vandergrift, Monica, viii

van der Vlugt, L. V., Van Nelle Factory, 150–151, 152, 162, *274*

Van Gelderen, Rosa, v

Vanna Venturi House, 41–42, *56*

Van Nelle Factory, 150–151, 152, 162, *274*

Venice, 111, *261, 262. See also specific works*

Venturi, Jim, v

Venturi, Robert, 115, 117, 118, 119, 145–146, 151, 177; *Complexity and Contradiction in Architecture,* 7–8, 13, 34, 73–74, 86, 118; *Learning from Las Vegas,* 8, 13, *20,* 34, 40, 41, 215; *Iconography and Electronics upon a Generic Architecture,* 8–9, 13; "The Beloved Las Vegas Strip of Yore," *21;* "Learning from Tokyo," *160. See also* VSBA

Verhaeren, Emile, "The Ship," 216

Vermeer, Jan, *A Young Woman Standing at a Virginal, 337*

Villa Savoye, *4,* 14, 41

Ville Radieuse, *9,* 15–16, *54, 55*

Vitruvius, 145–146, 151

Vuoksenniska church, 81, *137, 138*

Warhol, Andy, *Campbell's Soup I,* 52

Wheaton, William, viii, 222

Whitehall Ferry Terminal, 2, 59–60, *97, 98, 303*

Whitney Museum of Art, 43, 46, 48, *61, 68, 73*

Wilkins, William, National Gallery, 99–100

Williams College, *268–273*

Willmott, Peter, 109

Wislocki House, 51

World Trade Center, *192*

Wren, Sir Christopher: Main Building, College of William and Mary, 36, *43;* St. Paul's Cathedral, London, 79, *125, 126;* St. Stephen's Walbrook, 79, *127*

Wright, Frank Lloyd, 7, 175, 177; Broadacre City, *10,* 16; Pittsburgh Point, 16; Guggenheim Museum, 161

Yale University, Anlyan Center for Medical Research and Education, 68, *112*

Young, Michael, 109

Zumthor, Peter, Kunsthaus Bregenz, *13*